CRACKING THE CODE OF POSSIBILITIES IN BUSINESS

The Evolution of a New Command in Business
in an Age of Creative Entrepreneurship

TAIWO FAJOLU

WESTBOW®
PRESS
A DIVISION OF THOMAS NELSON
& ZONDERVAN

WestBow Press books may be ordered through booksellers or by contacting:

WestBow Press
A Division of Thomas Nelson & Zondervan
1663 Liberty Drive
Bloomington, IN 47403
www.westbowpress.com
1 (866) 928-1240

Because of the dynamic nature of the Internet, any web addresses or links contained in this book may have changed since publication and may no longer be valid. The views expressed in this work are solely those of the author and do not necessarily reflect the views of the publisher, and the publisher hereby disclaims any responsibility for them.

Any people depicted in stock imagery provided by Thinkstock are models, and such images are being used for illustrative purposes only. Certain stock imagery © Thinkstock.

ISBN: 978-1-4908-3244-9 (sc)
ISBN: 978-1-4908-3245-6 (hc)
ISBN: 978-1-4908-3243-2 (e)

Library of Congress Control Number: 2014905985

Printed in the United States of America.

WestBow Press rev. date: 04/24/2014

Cracking the Code of Possibilities in Business

"This book is a must read, particularly by the budding entrepreneurs. It is loaded with viable information, aimed at achieving practical and result oriented actions for developmental and growth objective in this aspect. Taiwo's effort in putting this book together is commendable. Let's utilize it productively."

-Otunba Ayan Kolawole
CEO, Kolaris Services Group Int'l, LLC (Enterprise & Manpower Development Consultants), Willingboro, New Jersey, USA

"'CRACKING THE CODE...' is a lively, pungent and intellectually stimulating excursion into how Nigeria can rediscover and reposition itself in the comity of nations through innovation, institutional renewal and reengineering, in an era of globalization. Absolutely un-put-down able."

-Dr Femi Orebe
Columnist, The Nation on Sunday

"It is very interesting, and for me interesting to understand more the African perspective. This is quite good, I enjoyed the content & style it is written in. I look forward to seeing it in print and to purchase a Signed Copy!"

-Kevin Bickerstaffe
Region Sales Manager (Middle East & Africa) UPS Products, ABB, UAE

"I must commend the efforts, intellect and insight Taiwo have put into this book. One of the most important elements of Nigeria or any country at allbecoming a great Nation is her Human Capabilities which makes Capacity Building a must. I will recommend that this book be used to teach in all Business Schools especially in ones that build and breed young Entrepreneurs ... Well Done."

-Gbenga Akinyombo
Executive Director, Subaru Motors Nigeria

"I find reading through 'Cracking the Code of Possibilities in Business' highly intellectual, stimulating and challenging. I have no hesitation in strongly recommending this book as a 'must-read' to all upcoming practicing young entrepreneurs who believe in the power of entrepreneurship to transform Africa. I also recommend the book to decision makers and opinion leaders who strive to identify the challenges facing entrepreneurs, and in pin-pointing the most trenchant barriers that inhibit high-impact entrepreneurship and in finding solution-driven dialogue in fostering high-impact entrepreneurship across the African continent."

-Abayomi Ojikutu
Charter President, Nigeria Institute of Management (2001-2003)

"I congratulate Taiwo Fajolu on this bold initiative. Although it didn't come to me as a surprise that he has joined the league of authors. Having read his seminal and scholarly contributions to Ekitipanupo, an intellectual roundtable we both belong; I saw it coming that it is a matter of time for a good book to come from his stable. He has a unique style of writing which places him in a class of his own. 'Cracking the Code of Possibilities in Business' is one book that anyone who has knack for originality and inclined to be inspired by fresh perspectives should read."

-Okan Seye Adetunmbi
Chief Responsibility Officer, Value Investing Limited, Nigeria

"This book is a brilliant effort in a multidisciplinary approach to a multisectoral development in a highly competitive and globalized world. I have no doubt that the author has exposed the contemplative and analytical segment of our society to a new vista, one that will massively impact us as a nation, this book is completely a fascinating work."

-Samson O.Ogundare
Controller Finance, Guardian Newspapers Ltd, Nigeria

"I have been opportuned to go through the book 'Cracking the Code ...' as authored by TaiwoFajolu, a thinker, philosopher, human resource manager, motivational speaker and author. The eight-chapter book delves extensively on engaging one's thinking faculty to drive best practices in business, identifying through the application of Vacuum Analysis, gaps in existing business structures, market and other commercial environments and developing systems to latch in on the vacuum so identified through the evolvement of new ideas. The author makes use of practical examples of radical business initiatives developed by change agents all over the world to draw home the point that uncommon progress could be recorded by thinking outside the box. He further alludes to the common saying that man can only be limited by his own vision and mission.This highly intellectual, extremely practical and thoughtful piece will definitely be a powerful tool of drawing the best of thinking process out of existing and new business executives, entrepreneurs, development economists, management consultants, academia and the industry generally. I have no hesitation whatsoever in recommending the book for the use of the identified interest groups and members of the larger society."

-Olusegun Ajibola (Ph.D., FCIB, FICA, LLB, BL)
The Director of Risk Management, Federal Inland Revenue Service (FIRS), and a former Executive Director and Regional Chief Executive, Intercontinental Bank now Access Bank (Nig) Plc

To my "code cracker," Edward

CONTENTS

FOREWORD

I T IS WITH pleasure that I write this foreword to this book written by Taiwo Fajolu. Taiwo was my student in the University of Lagos more than ten years ago. I have watched him grow intellectually since then. He has written a thought provoking book, even though I do not totally agree with everything said therein. But there is no doubt that since 9/11 the world has changed. Even before that time, globalization was upon us. His study of the lives of the giants of Western industries and eliciting lessons from their lives is of utmost relevance to a world suffering from the boom and burst and the cycle of growth and depression characteristic of Western economy.

This book is presumably written for young people in the developing world and I'm sure young people in the depressed economies of the Western world would also benefit from it. I hope this book will be very successful and all those who read it could benefit from it.

Professor Emeritus Akinjide Osuntokun (OON)
Former Ambassador of Nigeria to Germany, and The Pro-Chancellor and Chairman of Council, Ekiti State University.

A s I was preparing in my room for the class the next day, as a facilitator for the government on training the trainers program on Sustainable Development and Millennium Development Goals (MDGs), in Bauchi, some thought began to pop into my mind on critical issues that could make both leaders of corporation and their most important asset, the human capital, become a tool of national socio-economic and political prosperity.

We need not take for granted that the human mind is a thought factory, and, it has been proven beyond reasonable doubt that man can create anything which he can imagine, considering that creative faculty is the communication link between the finite mind and infinite intelligence. And through this, man has discovered and harnessed more of nature's forces.

Thus, all we need to do is train our creative faculty to believe big and be ambitious.

It was in view of the foregoing that I went into a 3-year research that birthed "Vacuum Analysis", a scientific approach towards value-driven competence development with an execution orientation. This technique was originally conceptualized to increase our availability skill, either as a staff member or an associate in an organization or as owner or manager of an enterprise. Here, a robust platform is created for us to be able to constantly evaluate and audit our performance on executed task, cultivate research skill, set achievable time bound goals, develop time management skills, be focused, and commit our vision to paper while setting goal around it, and the need to leverage organizational performance with the discipline of getting things done.

Nonetheless, it became established in my mind during this process that the concern of competence cannot be achieved ex-nihilo without being tied to the need for organizations, institutions, and individuals to tap into the resources made available through globalization. It was needful for me to make clear that we are in the regime of the flattened-world platform that ensures a new mechanism that provides a platform for velocity, farther, faster, deeper and even cheaper ways of executing task: And here, the tools and ability to connect, compete and collaborate with various economic forces and circumstances is made possible, where, anybody can connect all the knowledge centers on the planet, giving rise to an era of prosperity, innovation and collaboration.

Besides, it also became imperative to consider the fundamental problems bedeviling the country, one of which is a phenomenon of inefficient institutions. This has led to deeply-rooted corruption that has consistently weakened the nation's potential for greatness; hence, we propose an innovative and sustainable cure for this malady as she launch-pad herself for economic and social repositioning. And, suffice to say, to be repositioned, the country and Africa as a whole need Vision, a lot of Courage, Objectivity in the midst of diversity, simplicity, a lot of sacrifice, purposeful patience, and a global outlook. We also made it clear that only a genuine competitive system tends to go along with a high degree of equity of opportunity.

Indeed, the critical tangent of success in this age are creativity, innovation, re-invention, and availability: and also that, if we deal decisively with the problem of inefficient institution while providing the platform for creative entrepreneurship to thrive, it would take a shorter time for the country or the continent, as it were, to arrive at her destination.

Taiwo Fajolu
Lagos, Nigeria

Everything Changed after 9/11

E VERYTHING CHANGED—THIS IS a quite unnerving yet undeniable fact, as pointed out by Tom Peters, an American writer on business management practices best known for *In Search of Excellence* (1982). He affirms, "That day brought home the fact that the next war would not involve a definitive battle against another great war machine. Instead, a long-into-the-future series of skirmishes with exceptionally elusive enemies would be our new fate. We used to know exactly where the Bad Guys were. And exactly how big their bazookas were. (Big mattered most.) Now we didn't know where they were… or who they were… or what they were armed with. (Box cutters as weapons of mass destruction?) All we know was their motive. A motive defined, unlike the motive of the Soviet Union throughout most of the Cold War, by fanaticism." (*Reimagine* 2003)

This is a clear-cut wake-up message from someone totally dissatisfied with business-as-usual policies, either in the domain of the global combative warfare—the height of which the United States' Pentagon vividly represents—or in the domain of the corporate world.

The 9/11 attacks constituted a clinical execution of seemingly impossible actions resulting in a massive global impact. Truth be told: business can never be the same again. It is crucial and highly imperative that the owners of corporate empires revisit their operational commands, their business tactics, and their intelligence. Nobody can really claim to be untouchable in this new massive global tirade on businesses. More so, this should be of serious concern to evolving economies, including most African nations. Business leaders are thus saddled with the task of unraveling the connections inherent in the global trends in the business world vis-à-vis the capacity to execute seemingly impossible project of thoughts and ideas. It's indeed the regime of the Third World War, and it is to this concern we now turn.

CHAPTER I

New Soldier, New Weapon

S EPTEMBER 11, 2013, marked the twelfth anniversary of the 9/11 terrorist attack on the United States—an attack with massive global implications. As the popular saying goes, when the United States sneezes, every other part of the world catches cold. The world has hitherto never been the same since the attack. The country planned a series of events in remembrance of the nearly three thousand people killed in the well-executed assaults by the al-Qaeda terrorist group.

Needless to say, the old adage that "time heals all wounds" is apparently far from the truth in the United States, even at the twelfth anniversary, as memories of the event still traumatize Americans today. One prominent reaction occurred when Terry Jones, a pastor in a small Florida church, burned copies of the Koran, Islam's holiest text, which infused red-hot political and emotional elements into the anniversary while sparking international outrage against the pastor. US president Barack Obama referred to the move as a monumentally terrible idea.

Popular opinion was that Jones's intended reaction had marred an occasion usually marked with solemnity and quiet reflections throughout the United States, even though debate ragging on plans to construct a mosque near the former site of the World Trade Center had ignited anti-Muslim passions among those who believe that all

Muslims, not just the extremists, hate Americans. In fact, a recent *Washington Post/ABC News* poll found that a third of Americans believe that mainstream Islam encourages violence against non-Muslims, while 54 percent view the religion as peaceful. Two-thirds also object to the mosque being built so close to what is now known as Ground Zero, now a sacred spot. It is therefore not surprising that President Obama retorted, regarding the pastor's action, "This is a recruitment bonanza for al-Qaeda." He said in an interview on ABC's *Good Morning America*, "If Terry Jones is listening, I hope he understands that what he is proposing to do is completely contrary to our values as Americans. That this country has been built on the notion of freedom and religious tolerance. And as a very practical matter, I just want him to understand that this stunt that he is talking about pulling could greatly endanger our young men and women who are in uniform."

All these experiences, views, and counter-views constitute the upshot of the successful execution of one of the mad projects of the al-Qaeda network—an event that is forcing a change on the operational values and cultures of all nations. The battle tactics and strategy have changed, and the weapons of warfare have by necessity been redesigned. The new regime of warfare, according to Thomas L. Friedman in his book *Longitudes and Latitudes,* is empowering more nations, allowing them to reach "farther, faster, deeper, and cheaper than ever before.

These new soldiers are being given the tools and ability to connect, compete, and collaborate with various economic forces and circumstances to emerge with new and dynamic weapons. This has resulted in a new mode of operation that changes the culture of doing business by allowing them to clinically execute virtually impossible tasks with an awesome level of coordination.

Needless to say, several battles have been fought throughout history between great political and economic empires—from Jerusalem to Athens, from Athens to Rome, from Rome to London, and from London to New York. These conflicts have resulted in battles like the ones between Zionists and non-Zionists in AD 1099, the Trojan War between the Greeks and the inhabitants of Troy, or that of the Marathon Battle, where about ten thousand Greeks were victorious over thirty thousand Persians.

These battles (and countless others) virtually transferred economic power from one empire to another or from one civilization to another. But no battle shows evidence of power being shifted into the hands of soldiers.

Similarly, people are now obtrusively connecting all knowledge centers on the planet into a single global network, which is strategically ushering in an era of prosperity, innovation, and collaboration by companies, communities, and individuals. Indeed, the *New York Times* Foreign Affairs columnist Thomas Friedman describes it best when saying his personal dread sprang from the obvious fact that it's not only the software writers and computer geeks who get empowered by connecting knowledge centers. Such collaboration is also available to al-Qaeda and other terrorist networks. According to Friedman, "The playing field is not being leveled only in ways that draw in and super-empower a whole new group of innovators. It's being leveled in a way that draws in a whole new group of angry, frustrated, and humiliated men and women."

Clearly, the sources of wealth evolving from the new command in the business world include software, brainpower, complex algorithms, knowledge workers, call centers, transmission protocols, and breakthroughs in optical engineering. These, among others, are the new weapons of the new soldiers, which are creating greater capacity for the outsourcing of services and information technology work from America and other industrialized countries. A practical example is the success story of one of the most respectable captains of industry in India, Nandan Nilekani, the CEO of Infosys Technologies Limited in Bangalore, India's own Silicon Valley. Here specific software programs are written, just like in the back rooms of major American- and European-based multinational companies "from maintenance to specific research projects to answering customer calls routed there from all over the world." Nilekani thus claims, according to Friedman, that Infosys "can hold a virtual meeting of the key players from its entire global supply chain for any project at any time on that super-sized screen. So their American designers could be on the screen speaking with their Indian software writers and their Asian manufacturers all at once."

It is important at this juncture that we juggle some data around and lay emphasis on the implications of these figures. This could be useful for this discourse as it is a fact that the strong continuation of long-term growth in the volume of international trade signals that the global economy is becoming ever more closely integrated, the global trade recession notwithstanding. As global trade grows faster than global GDP, national economies are becoming increasingly intertwined, depending on each other for ever-larger percentages of goods and services. As this development continues to unfold, the emerging economies of Asia and Africa stand in a vantage position to benefit more than ever. In this connection, countries like Nigeria are afforded the privilege to jump-start their economies as globalization keeps accelerating with global markets and their national production systems in tow. The concomitant benefit of this development is greater trade translating into increased efficiency in the world economy, income gains in countries involved in the global trading system, and greater global economic growth.

In 1999, a United Nations survey revealed that enterprises based in one country invested some $860 billion in productive assets in another country. This was up from $732 billion in 1998. "To put it in perspective, in 1980 the value of foreign direct investment was just $60 billion, and in 1990 it was $210 billion."[1] (*Global Business Today* 2002)

The rapid expansion in foreign direct investment (FDI) suggests two things. First, individual enterprises are increasingly building global production systems, dispersing various activities to those locations in the world where they can be produced most efficiently. Second, the data implies that enterprises are entering each other's markets in an attempt to create and exploit emerging global markets for the goods and services they produce. Besides the prosperity being exchanged through the outsourcing of services, some data also suggests a massive rise in the volume and value of cross-border mergers and acquisitions. Suffice it to say that mergers and acquisitions, rather than building operations from the ground up, are becoming the favored mode of entering foreign markets. "In 1999, for example, the value of completed cross-border mergers and acquisitions rose to $720 billion and involved about 6,000 transactions, up from $100 billion in 1987" (Charles W. L. Hill, *International Business: Competing In The Global Marketplace* 2002, 4). And as a result of foreign direct investment activity, there were some 63,000 multinational companies in the world as of 2002, with about 700,000 foreign affiliates.

Sadly, prior to this time the poorer nations of the world were being left on the sidelines in the headlong rush toward global economic integration. Africa, for example, had accounted for a little more than 1 percent of all foreign direct investment in 1999 and about 2 percent of all international trade flows. The World Bank had focused on this issue, noting that one-sixth of the world's people produce 78 percent of the world's goods and services and receives 78 percent of the world's income, representing countries like the United States, the United Kingdom, France, Germany, the Netherlands, China, and Mexico. Incongruously, "Three-fifth of the world's people in the sixty-one poorest countries receive 6 percent of the world's income," the bank disclosed (*Global Business Today* 2002).

As at 2002, the continuing disparity had suggested that one of the biggest challenges facing global economic institutions such as the World Trade Organization, the World Bank, the International Monetary Fund, and the United Nations was how to bring the poorer nations of the world into the global economic system of the twenty-first century and that the exclusion of the majority of the world's population from the global economic system represents an enormous waste of resources. Indeed if the lot of the poor does not improve, the growing division between the rich and poor nations of the world could lead to geopolitical conflicts that impinge on the economic prosperity of the developed world.

Obviously, at the time in consideration, power and prosperity filtered into the hands of some wrong and frustrated soldiers, such as the al-Qaeda, resulting in devastating reactions worse than the geopolitical conflict that had ensued. The battle strategy has changed; armored tanks are being substituted with information, and the prevailing concern is about future combat systems being fought with software rather than tanks and artillery; this is a situation where, for example, manufacturing operations in the old economy engages information, turning it into a solutions-strategy to meet customers' needs.

Friedman makes the point clearer when he opined that there have been three great eras of globalization: "Globalization 1.0 was about countries and muscle. That is, in Globalization 1.0, the key agent of change, the dynamic force driving the process of global integration, was how much brain—how much muscle, how much horsepower, wind power, or, later, steam power—your country had and how creatively you could deploy it" (*The World Is Flat* 2005).

He further affirms:

> The second great era, Globalization 2.0, lasted roughly from 1800 to 2000, interrupted by the Great Depression and world wars I and II. This era shrank the world from a size medium to a size small. In Globalization 2.0, the key agent of change, the dynamic force driving global integration, was multinational companies. These multinationals went global for markets and labor, spearheaded first by the expansion of the Dutch and English joint-stock companies and the Industrial Revolution.

He maintains:

> Around the year 2000 we entered a whole new era: Globalization 3.0. Globalization 3.0 is shrinking the world from a size small to a size tiny and flattening the

playing field at the same time. And while the dynamic force in Globalization 1.0 was countries globalizing and the dynamic force in Globalization 2.0 was companies globalizing, the dynamic force in Globalization 3.0-the force that gives it its unique character-is the newfound power for individuals to collaborate and compete globally. And the phenomenon that is enabling, empowering, and enjoining individuals and small groups to go global so easily and so seamlessly is what I call the flat-world platform …

Such platform, as in Globalization 3.0, confers massive-unlimited capacity to individuals who cares to be courageous enough to own his or her content in digital form, as offered unto them by the tools that personal computers make available, through fiber optic cable and the advancement in the parameters of workflow software, granting them access to increasingly huge digital content at little or no cost as well as enabling them to collaborate on the same from anywhere, the distance notwithstanding.

The emphasis here is that beyond the cutthroat competition among businesses around the world, there is a wider network of platforms upon which individuals could tap into one another's exposures and experiences, either cognitive or emotional, in order to form a formidable force in the share of the global economic value and innovation. The kind of vocation or enterprise we engage in does not really matter here; what matter is that there is a greater opportunity for all who will be bold enough to take calculated risks in any economic endeavor that will bring prosperity and increase the value being created everywhere in the world today.

A good point of departure is to take progressive actions and make definite decisions, articulating further plans on the business in which you are already established. You must refocus your business with a bold impression on yourself and the people you transact with, according to which there is no more limitation in the global field. We are in a time of limitless opportunities! The "Red Sea" has been parted for all to cross. Now, nothing can stop whomever makes a courageous and creative attempt to cross this new ocean of stupendous opportunity and become free from primordial barriers, moving into inexhaustible prosperity that is being afforded all.

All humans desire to extend their horizon to capture every opportunity available. These opportunities are developed through the natural search and yearning for more food, more clothes, better shelter, more luxury, more beauty, more knowledge, and more pleasure. Our creative ability and capacity for enterprise get energized and motivated the moment we have the assurance that nothing is going to stifle our ability to extend beyond limits. It is not improper to affirm that the progressive course of globalization is an evolutionary process that demands every living thing is under obligation to make continuous advancement. The moment any human enterprise or institution is able to put an end to the capacity of humans to evolve new ways of life or system or inhibit the capacity or possibility to explore the uncharted courses, then the end of all things has come. More so, it is important for every man and woman, every business and institution to prosper and proceed into abundant life even as they create economic value in the land. It is important to grab with vigor and tenacity the opportunity being created by the new global trend in the world of business, where no one is really denied the capacity to plug in to the real arena of life devoid of any cage or barrier that had once been created by the prosperous nations of Euro-America (of both European and American ancestry).

Besides, one of the best ways to enter into abundant life in this regime of global commerce and enterprise is for individuals or individual groups to see themselves as the creative center from which increase is distributed to all. As each person penetrates deeply into the inexhaustible global port of stupendous wealth, prosperity, power, and opportunities, he or she must explore and exploit and indeed turbo-charge his or her creative ability. Each, to this end, should create highly innovative products for the sake of efficiency and for high economic value—that is, products that are bankable and also give customers full value for their money, as well as give them the impression of increase.

It is important that every business owner and the would-be business owner create the impression of an advancing person in their actions, endeavors, and transactions until they get inspired and allow this to permeate in such a way that the delivery of the product offers another the chance of enjoying the benefits of the new world order of limitless opportunities. Everyone having this concern must become impressive and remain consistently so, such that anyone who has a transaction with you would receive a use-value greater than the cash-value you are receiving from them. In doing this, you create a moment of light and will scarcely lack customers. This is because people will naturally gravitate toward where they are given the impression of increase, and as you deliver this, regardless of your type of business, they will locate you, to the tremendous advantage of your business. This will give you the opportunity to increase your leading edge and give you a wider market space. Indeed, the global space has more than enough to bless everyone without going bankrupt.

Nonetheless, it is germane to note that several civilizations prior to now, many nations, and owners of business empires have been seduced by the greedy accumulation of wealth and power and have used these to extend their dominion by bloody battles and devastating their economy. But then, we are in a regime that empowers one and all, and no one can really lay claim to any superior power over the other. Our calling is to focus our creative ability and hold on to our visions, not losing sight of our purpose in life.

This concern is better laid bare by the moral derived from the life of Samuel Milton, who says, "What I want for myself, I want for everybody."

> Samuel Milton Jones was born in 1846 in Ty Mawr Bedd, Gelert, in North Wales. As a small boy, he immigrated to

the eastern United States with his parents. After starting out in the then-new oil industry in Pennsylvania and following its westward expansion, he began manufacturing oilfield drilling equipment in Toledo, Ohio, in 1894.

He soon earned a reputation for honest business and for fair dealings with the workers in his employ. The story goes that he said his factory needed only one policy—the well-known Golden Rule ("Do unto others as you would have them do unto you")—and he dramatically nailed a plaque with that phrase to the factory wall. As an employer, he was ahead of his time, a true maverick who "walked his talk." Workers at his factory enjoyed eight-hour working day (instead of the usual ten), a one-week vacation, paid holidays, insurance, plus a park and playground. He also did away with bosses and timekeepers and held employee picnics.

Toward the end of 1800s he became mayor of Toledo and served four terms, becoming the city's most respected and popular political leader and achieving fame across the nation and around the world.

As mayor, he championed the public park system and public ownership of utilities. He also replaced policemen's nightsticks with walking sticks and refused to prosecute so-called "morality laws," which he felt were unfair to the poor.

Applying his principle to his business and political endeavors earned him immense respect and affection as well as his nickname. In 1904, at the age of fifty-seven, Mr. Jones died suddenly while still in office. Not surprisingly, his funeral was said to be the largest and best attended in the city's history.

It's important to mention at this juncture that there is something about the "truth": you can't improve on the truth, you cannot upgrade the truth, you cannot modernize the truth, you cannot civilize the truth, you can only employ and deploy the truth if you so choose; and the truth in respect of this concern is that every man in business must have a mission of how he wants to impact the world in a positive way, and to do this requires tremendous *focus*. This is because focus often leads to a fuller, richer, and satisfying life. It makes you understand the "time matrix" and how your choices affect your life; it helps you to discover your governing values, those things that really matter most to you; and you will be able to start the process of having short- and long-term goals; you will learn the system of effective prioritizing and execution of those goals.

The needs of mankind keep changing, and solutions are being demanded on a consistent basis. It is thus absolutely imperative that every business determine what their highest priorities are in line with their vision and the specific mission to produce economically innovative solutions to human needs. Every business must have a mission, and it's important it stays with its mission if its promoter doesn't want to be a victim of frustration. Your mission is like carrying the staff of Moses, which has the capacity to deliver nations; you must value it greatly. It's like a little light: you must let it shine, even if it does not appeal to your competition, inasmuch as it follows what Jim Collins called the Hedgehog Concept (three overlapping circles; see Figure 1) in his book *Good to Great: Why Some Companies Make the Leap … and Others Don't* (2002). You will have to operate by clear-cut instructions in line with your mission.

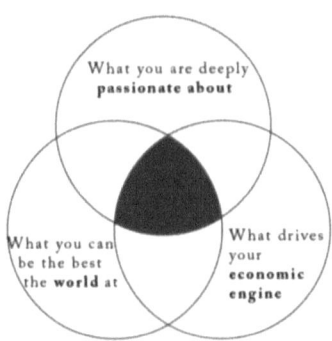

Figure 1

It is important that we acquire the tools and skills needed in order to build the capacity to focus on the highest priorities of our mission, manage our time, and lead better lives. This comes with being single minded. Those who walk, walk with many; those who run, run with a few; but those who fly, fly alone. Walking requires only common sense, while running requires principles, but flying demands instruction. That's why teachers in flying schools are not called professors but instructors.

Now, there is no school teaching a child how to walk. Every average child learns how to walk by human nature. He naturally takes one step after another, and there is no certificate for this course or license to practice it. You know that driving does not merely entail common sense; you must know the principles (and that's why advanced countries in Europe and America pay greater attention to how you learned to drive than to your marriage). No amount of improvisation can convert the motor into a steering wheel; nor can you use the brake as clutch. So there are principles you must follow to drive. But to fly, it's not just principle, it's instruction: if you don't press this button at this particular time, then you might be headed to the great beyond if you did not feel like following instruction. Life is a school, and we must teach ourselves to glean what will help us understand where we are going.

Besides, the core concern of this discourse won't have been fully addressed without one emphasizing that it is imperative to focus our time, energy, and values on those things that are of most importance in our mission.

Here, in "The Runaround Dilemma," an anonymous author muses:

> Because we don't know what is really important to us, everything seems important.
>
> Because everything seems important, we have to do everything.

Other people, unfortunately, see us as doing everything, so they expect us to do everything.

Doing everything keeps us so busy, we don't have time to think about what is really important to us.

It is not about "the show horse" but "the plow horse." It is about a simple and missionary lifestyle, leading a courageous life to take an organization from a low point and transform it into a great one. It is about putting hand to work with a specific goal and mission in mind, that even though it won't come easy and quick, you will eventually arrive at a safe haven.

Such was the stupendous courage and boldness mixed with humility and simplicity of Ken Iverson, the CEO who oversaw the transformation of Nucor from near bankruptcy to one of the most successful steel companies in the world, driving it up to a Fortune 500 company.

When the entire American steel industry was facing severe challenges in the 1970s, and big corporations like Bethlehem Steel where complaining and blaming the problem on the importation of cheap steel into the country, the Nucor executives, led by Ken Iverson, viewed the problem as the failure of management to keep pace with innovation. Indeed, it was recorded that when Nucor's transformation started in 1965, the company, formerly Nuclear Corporation of America, did not produce one ounce of steel, nor did it make a penny of profit.

But then the transformation started. It involved the promotion of one of their general managers to CEO; getting the right people onboard with him; and giving him the freedom to build his own remarkable team. The CEO set forth on a mission of building a great company, even though he refused to explain how to get there but rather engaged in a Socratic dialectics in several series of purposeful arguments and debates among the management team. Thirty years later, Nucor stood as the fourth-largest steel maker in the world as at 2001 when *Good to Great* was published.

As far as the Nucor executives were concerned, the way forward consisted in an atmosphere of intense dialogue, loud debate, heated discussions, and healthy conflict without anybody taking the subject of discourse personal. Those discussions were not engaged in for the fun of it nor to make you succumb to a predetermined decision. The process was more like a heated scientific debate, with people engaged in a search for the best answers.

Nucor at the onset was indeed not regarded a great industrial outfit, yet that did not deter them from building a system with a clinical understanding of what the key drivers in their economic engine were. They had the clarified and simplified mission of becoming the best at harnessing culture and technology to produce low-cost steel, taking advantage of their skill in creating a performance culture and taking "farsighted bets" on new manufacturing technologies. Again, despite the fact that Nucor was among the "bottom 5 percent" of industries, they beat the market by well more than five times. This did not happen by members of the Nucor team yelling and screaming at each other in heated debates until solution towards the transformation emerged.

CHAPTER 2

Vacuum Analysis

WITHOUT DOUBT, MANY corporations in Nigeria, Egypt, South Africa, and other parts of Africa are expanding and in step with the global trends. From their various headquarters down to their subsidiaries and other branches and outlets of the organizations, the trend is becoming increasingly apparent. Several CEOs, who are the main custodians of their corporations' vision and mandate, have continued to marshal commands to their troops in the organizations and demand consistent feedback from general managers, supervisors, and other officers. They have a duty to ensure adherence to the course of the vision and mission of the organization. Many of these organizations are indeed being held together by the strength of the leadership. Most of the corporate leaders operate like generals in the army, especially in the banking sector.

However, more often than not, the reality on ground is that there is a huge lacuna in the level of competence among members of staff of these organizations, despite witnessing the revolutionary changes being brought about by some of their very smart directors with global exposure. The concern here demands improved competence far from the usual and a totally new approach to business in order to be able to operate at the same level of speed with the new leadership.

It is thus the responsibility of every staff member to stand up to the task by exhibiting pragmatic qualities in respect to skills, increased confidence, and high productivity. Hence, it is imperative for the "human capital" (or members of staff, as it were) under this new direction to prove that they are not ducks but are high-flying eagles. It is for this purpose that a "vacuum analysis technique" is required for measuring and developing the level of competence and productive performance of the human capital of these organizations.

The benefits from adopting this technique include

- Increasing one's market value as individuals
- Becoming more productive and creative
- Increasing one's confidence on the job and in life overall
- Having reasons to operate with more commitment, diligence, and integrity
- Becoming one's own boss of sorts within the domain of operation and taking ownership by being responsible in the handling of duties
- Improving the possibilities of exploring one's idle capacity
- Improving oneself as a quality brand by benchmarking the best in the industry; and
- Being a headliner in the repositioning of the organization as a high flier in performance, accountability, integrity, purposeful creativity, and in exploring any form of idle capacity for tremendous profitability.

It is imperative at this juncture to consider what a vacuum is before we begin to unravel the yarn. A vacuum is an empty physical space or an absence of matter. In common parlance, vacuum is a volume of space that is essentially empty of matter. From the study of quantum physics, the classical notion of a perfect vacuum with gaseous pressure of exactly zero is only a philosophical concept and is never observed in practice. Physicist often discuss ideal test results that would occur in a perfect vacuum, while they simply call vacuum a "free space" and use the term "partial vacuum" to refer to a real vacuum.

The word vacuum comes from the Latin term *in vacuo* which is used to describe an object as empty. Vacuum has been a frequent topic of philosophical debate since Ancient Greek times, but was not studied empirically until the seventeenth century, when Evangelista Torricelli produced the first laboratory vacuum in 1643, and other experimental techniques were developed as a result of his theory of atmospheric pressure. Vacuum became a valuable industrial tool in the twentieth century with the introduction of incandescent light bulbs and vacuum tubes. A wide array of vacuum technology has since become available. The recent development of human space flight has also raised interest in the impact of vacuum on human health, and on life forms in general. This gives credence to the saying that "Nature abhors a vacuum," yet there is so much wisdom in the philosophy of vacuum.

Again, it is interesting that in the enterprise of human capacity building, the theory of vacuum is being established by some, including this writer. This obviously would have been to the amazement of Evangelista Torricelli himself.

What Is Vacuum Analysis?

The vacuum analysis approach as a scientific technique and a critical way of measuring competence, which is value-driven and execution-oriented. This, as well as confidence on the job, is to be derived from its etymological or original sense, *in vacuo*, as used to describe an object as empty.

The question relevant to this concern is: What emptiness do you create when or if you are moved away from your table or work station? Is there any significant impact created by you to such an extent that pulling you away from that space creates so much vacuum, such emptiness, that the space has proved difficult to fill even though those who were asked to replace you are supposed to have competence in the same line of duty? Have you branded yourself so much that it would be difficult for five people to fill your shoe? Is your work rate so high that when you left the last table, your boss suddenly realized they would need five people to occupy the position you just left?

This is the crux of our discourse.

Suffice to say that vacuum analysis is therefore an approach for measuring individual or group competence, level of work rate, confidence on the job, the cerebral influence of each person or group or each person in a group on a particular task, and the ability to execute projects within the given time.

What percentage of your Intelligent Quotient (IQ), Emotional Quotient (EQ), and Social Intelligence have you applied on your duty or job in such a way that when your boss gives you a task, his heart does not palpitate in fear of your not delivering to the uttermost? What guarantee does he have that if your work is evaluated, it would meet nothing but excellent remarks?

Now it is critical to consider that it is sometime possible for you to fool your boss by cleverly hiding your incompetence, or that the reason he still keeps you around is either because he has not found a good alternative or because he is so kind he doesn't want to create chaos in your family and throw them off balance by committing you back to the labor market. It is also likely he doesn't want to rock the boat and create panic in the system. Nor is he trying to manage you and encourage you now and then to work harder and smarter with the hopes that you will get better.

But then, it would be difficult for you to fool an external reviewer as you are likely to unravel before him or her considering he or she is probably going to be more objective. Or why do you think a lot of people, and more so accountants, are usually not comfortable with external auditors?

For instance, in higher institutions, where serious cerebral tasks are being performed, it has occurred on many occasions where students' grades following an exam or completion of research work could be radically reduced following the intervention of an external examiner, a common practice among examiners in Africa's higher institutions of learning.

An incident occurred a few years back while pursuing my first degree, involving a particular lecturer nicknamed The G (meaning Genius). He was a senior lecturer whose specialty was logic, critical thinking, and philosophy of science. He came in sometime to lecture us on logic after, as it appeared, he might have drank a bottle of vodka. He would teach with such overwhelming brilliance that you could never keep up with him. I took pride in being regarded as the only person who could catch up, and my notes became essential commodity in my class. Nationwide, everybody knows he does a thorough job in overseeing students' theses. However, many students consider him a "fatal accident" and dread him more than the Devil. Anytime they found out he had been appointed to be their final year project supervisor, they would usually whine and do all they could to avoid him. Indeed, many students ended up with poor grades in their final year because they focused all their attention to pleasing him in their theses to such extent that they hardly could prepare well for their final exams. Hence, the need for external supervisor became a superfluity insofar as it was this lecturer who did the initial supervision of a given project, as he was known for his thoroughness.

The above illustration points to the fact that although your boss may yet encounter your level of competence and work rate, can this productivity level of yours stand the test of the crucible of fire from a highly cerebral external assessor? Or is it that you make your boss so afraid that his heart starts beating faster than normal anytime he discovers external assessors are coming to review your department?

You should begin to ask yourself what your impact here is. Have you improved on your expertise or knowledge and become so dependable that even if you were not next in line on the hierarchy, would your boss choose another person to replace him in his absence—or would you be his choice? Or if he desired sending someone out to represent him in a high-profile meeting, would he think of you as an intelligent option, or would he think it a fatal flaw to choose you?

Again, if you are moved out of the system, what vacuum, what emptiness would you create that would be difficult to fill by another? Is your work rate that high such that would be difficult for another person or even group of persons to operate in the same capacity without your intervention?

Considering some of your colleagues who have left the organization or have been redeployed to other stations, how many do you still consult individually or as a group?

It's high time you started measuring your competence level with this vacuum analysis technique so as not to be caught unawares when such measure is applied on you by your manager or an unattached external supervisor. Once your case is such that you develop palpitations or get incredibly agitated anytime you hear an external supervisor is on the way to review your work, there is a serious problem indeed.

DEVELOPING COMPETENCE THROUGH VACUUM ANALYSIS TECHNIQUE

Having explained what vacuum analysis is, it's important we consider how to apply the same approach to develop your level of competence within your operational domain so as to aid the execution of your job with high performance to the satisfaction of your boss or head of the department.

Given a workplace scenario where there is a chain of command and staff with varying levels of exposure and experience, in order to experience corporate development in terms of competence, each departmental head would have to work to ensure that his or her department considers the need to improve its level of competence and by extension confidence as highly important.

Although the job may be intertwined across departments, let it be so glaring that your department is the leader in the field in such a way that your subordinates would be proud to be operating under your leadership.

Everyone must critically consider his or her line of duty and begin to take pragmatic steps toward improving in each of those lines by consistently carrying out a review of how far you have improved within determined parameters.

In order to do this you need to consistently carry out enormous research. You need to consistently have a meeting with yourself and ask questions about how to develop your level of competence so you could stand in for your boss while he's away, and by extension become his lab of intelligence and creativity.

It's imperative that you begin to turn in-and-out every fiber of your talents and potential in relation to your line of duty so as to improve your capacity to deliver with high level of accuracy within a timeline.

You should consider how you brand your department within the structure of command and mandate given to you such that your department becomes so unique in terms of integrity, rate of performance in execution of any task at all, and the capacity for excellent delivery of your deliverables.

You should begin to consider how you can strategically position your department such that even your boss cannot but wonder how you got the job done with such accuracy and within the given time limits.

You should consider how you would entrench your department in the organization such that you become indispensable. Hence, should the organization ever consider scrapping or dislodging your department out of the system, it would amount to it erasing itself. This is because over time, it has evolved into becoming your organization's lifeline and success story.

There is the need to intelligently fashion a smart model and module of operation that should make it almost impossible for any other department to operate without having to consult you. You have to leverage and transcend your present performance and give your boss cause to wonder. You need to lift your banner so high with an improved ability to dissolve doubts and design solutions to problems inherent in any task. You must improve on promoting the image of the organization by way of carrying out your duties more efficiently and effectively.

As a team operating in a particular department, you must operate a well-structured, well-managed system that boosts confidence, improves competence, and rides on the wings of integrity aimed at achieving greater attainment of set objectives for the progress of the organization.

LEVERAGING ORGANIZATIONAL PERFORMANCE

The concern here discusses what to do to improve the performance level of the organization from the perspective of the head of a team or department.

We aim to take a close assessment of team heads or heads of department in relation to their subordinates in pursuant to the goal of having optimal productivity, performance, and profitability in the organization. Hence the need to raise the following questions arise in order for us to get a good grasp of the task we are saddled with.

As the head of a team or department, members of your team are your "internal customers." It is highly important to your operation that you define your role in the scheme of things. The relevant questions include

- Are you a team player?
- Do you involve your team collaboratively to make decisions?
- Do you provide your team materials needed for expeditious work?
- Do you display any negative attitude that is affecting their overall efficiency?
- Do you lose your temper?
- Is the morale of your team dropping because of your attitude?
- Has the commitment to the job become tenuous because of you?

- What negative impact have your actions or inactions caused to individual or corporate performance?
- Is the operational atmosphere of your group a contentious one?
- Are you by your attitude breeding a group of non-team players?
- Is there a clear understanding regarding what the rules are within your team, especially in respect of resource allocation?
- Are your team members competing for resources?
- Is anybody short-changed on your team?
- Are there complaints on your team? If so, have you analyzed those complaints?
- Is there internal rivalry within and among different groups in their interrelationships?
- Is there a culture of resentment and/or blame?
- What strategy are you using to help your group work out its issues?
- Are there gripes among the team member?
- What strategy are you using to create a new culture of decorum?
- Are you a person of vision?
- What is your vision for your team?
- What is your strategy to help build a more positive internal environment?
- What positive initiative are you embarking upon?
- Are you engaging your team in order to decide together?
- How are you and your team working to produce solutions together?
- How are you confronting your own personality and emotions and taking responsibility for your group?
- Do you have a good grasp of the use of the key levers of support needed for change?
- What effort are you making to ensure that your team is committed to working as a group?
- How is your response to work affecting the bottom line of the organization?
- What information are you bringing to your team to build the individual capacity of your team?

- Are you a team builder?
- Are you evolving any transformational model to improve your team?
- What effort are you making to re-invent your group?
- Do you take things for granted?
- Do you take people for granted?
- Are you an inspirational leader in your team?
- What are the things you are doing to show that you are determined to seeing your organization become a winning brand?
- What superior values are you as a superior officer instilling in your subordinate?
- How do you inspire and mentor your subordinates?
- How are you encouraging your subordinates to perform better?
- What would be the rate of your performance if you are to be evaluated on your success in nurturing, encouraging, and mentoring your subordinates?

Indeed, should you pay close attention to the questions hitherto, and you work hard to integrate your answers into your work, what you will get is a working environment charged with excitement, creative energy, and commitment. Note also that if you are the best, anything is possible for you, and you can be the best if you are willing to make a total commitment to this end.

For the company to be an excellent organization, there must be an intentional breeding of staff that strives to be the best. This is a tall order for all the staff members with subordinates. It is by clinically following through with these concerns and executing them in your daily processes that you will make the mandate given to your boss an easier one to fulfill.

Besides, there is need for a purposeful synergy within the organization. The organization itself is an organism whose survival depends on the quality of interrelationships and interdependence of departments or units of duties. When this is properly integrated into the culture of your operation in line with your vision and purpose, it will naturally lead to the strengthening and growth of the organization, and there should be a consistent review of your work and operations to this effect.

You must take into serious consideration that the business environment is constantly changing. Nobody can predict with certainty the next thing that will happen to your industry or the sector in which your organization operates. Any pronouncement can come from the government regulators, which would demand your compliance. So you could be in serious trouble if your mind is not prepared to readily adapt to change.

If you have not raised the required standard of competence and the confidence needed in your operational model either as individual or department or organization, you may run into a dire situation if an unexpected change is decreed by forces beyond your control.

According to Newton's first law of gravity, change in the form of a massive force can only be resisted to your own peril. An organization is poised to assume competitive leadership of its industry when it demonstrates the readiness to adjustment and accept change as a revealer of opportunities.

BENCHMARKING AGAINST THE BEST (THE IMPERATIVENESS OF IMPROVING ONE'S PERFORMANCE)

This is a call to reinvent the individual you. The history of Egypt and the development of Europe through the Grecian Emperor Alexander the Great, who was a student of Aristotle, is relevant to this discourse on the need to continue self-reinvention by way of permanent self-improvement to become the best in one's chosen endeavor.

Alexander the Great continued his father's exploits in conquering the whole Mediterranean, after which he devised a robust strategy for conquering the world, especially the first civilization in history, Egypt. Most of the earliest philosophers of great repute had visited

Egypt and recorded her to be a place of thriving learning woven in mysticism and guarded by the priesthood. Alas! Alexander the Great would invade Egypt just like he did many other empires, and Egypt would never be the same.

The prime target, I presume, of the Grecian emperor was the Egyptian library, being a man of immense interest in learning as he was himself being tutored from childhood by Aristotle, one of the world's most renowned Philosophers, whose Syllogistic logic was the canon for about 150 years. Thus, the Egyptian library was seized and the priests forced to interpret the mystical yet highly scientific works, which were subsequently delivered to Europe via the Greeks.

Aristotle was the first to lay hold on this vast cornucopia of knowledge. He had studied under Plato for twenty years. Aristotle began work on this platform of great and deep knowledge and wisdom; and ever since then, Europe and indeed the whole of the Western world, have never been the same. This is why it appeared Aristotle had something to say on every field of human endeavor and enterprise.

Europe has since continued to reinvent herself!

You are the storyteller of your own life, and you can decide to create your own legend. There is nothing worse than remaining ordinary. Make sure you desist from pampering your lack of performance on your job. Think of it this way: you've got a new boss—the new boss is you.

There is, therefore, the need for you to benchmark yourself against the best in every aspect of your duty within your operational domain vis-à-vis the global market. It is highly imperative you take ownership of your domain by wisdom, knowledge, improved skills, understanding, and integrity. You must unleash the individual in you. We are in the age of creativity, and intensification is not a chimera, nor is it a figment of the imagination.

In the United States now, the creative class already encompasses more than thirty-eight million people, or 30 percent of the workforce, and the impact is massive (*Re-Imagine* 2003).

Professor Richard Florida, a protagonist of creativity, affirms that creativity is the driving force of economic growth. He also claims that the creative class has become dominant in the America society of today.

As an individual, you will have to reinvent yourself. The world is changing in respect of value proposition and trend shifting. Now the nations of the world in the last one hundred years have treated their territory as a closed system. Their goals is to make the lives of their citizens better within the confines of that territory.

However, that autarchic trend among modern nation-states is no longer tenable because the imperatives of a global economy, as well as globalism, have overwhelmed that possibility. The mantle of governance is shifting from the mostly autonomous "nation-state" to the globally interdependent "market-state."

In line with this shift, former US president Bill Clinton, during his regime, strongly affirmed that "in a global economy, the government cannot give anybody a guaranteed success story but you can give people the tools to make the most of their own lives."

This is what your organization should do for you through your CEO: give you the tools to make the most of your life. It now behooves you to respond intensely, intelligently, and indeed creatively with a high level of integrity to utilize to full capacity the tools handed over to you for the improvement of your competence within your job description, or in any other thing you are either instructed to do or that you ever find yourself doing. For it is in doing this that you make the most of your life even as the organization fulfills its own obligation by paying your salary.

This is all about *attitude*.

Your attitude to pragmatic response to change is being challenged here. Is your attitude to change in this respect a response to changes forced down your throat? Or are you excited about the change and have aligned yourself to it in such a way that it improves your taste, levitates your passion, improves your competence, and increases your confidence?

Again, one word that has relevance to the all-important subject of you benchmarking yourself against the best in line with the need to improve your performance is the word "branding." Branding as a perennially serious subject in business circles today is being used as a marketing tool for selling a product or service. But in this discourse, branding is an "attitude" issue.

It is a question of what lies within my soul. The question you might want to ask: How can I become a brand in this organization—a brand prompt on deliverables; a brand with the swiftest and best detailed feedback system; a brand of integrity; a brand of confidence; a smart and highly intelligent response on instructions and duty?

When you develop yourself as a strong brand, you make your organization a strong brand amongst its contemporaries in the industry.

Let us not continue with the attitude of taking things for granted. Needless to say, you are a brand, like Coca-Cola, Microsoft, or Google. The question is: What is your brand *equity*? Is the value high or low? Growing or declining? Solid or fragile?

It is of great importance for you to build yourself a high-quality, growing, and strong brand by proactively carrying out your duties with intelligence and integrity and great humility. As you do this, you will find that you will have increased your market value.

EXPLOITING MY IDLE CAPACITY

The point of departure for this concern is the assumption that when you do more, you earn more, and you will invariably be more. However, the fact that you do more does not mean you will earn more or that you would become more fulfilled in life. In fact, you could become "Jack of many trades and master of none," especially if you don't pay serious attention to the suggestions here.

This is particularly designed to help you focus your energy on the real deal in your private affairs, in order for you to be able to exploit your "idle capacity" (the remaining amount of capacity left in a company after productive capacity and protective capacity have been eliminated from consideration) to profit. It would also aid you in having a more fulfilling life in the real sense of it and by extension play your role effectively with joy and happiness, increased level of confidence, and enlarged capacity for competence within the value chain point you occupy in your organization.

In considering, for instance, a factory as a complex synchronization of resources, human and material, which processes input into a throughput to give an output, efficiency is not the measure of the success of a factory but profitability. In other words, the essence of business is not efficiency but profitability. A factory can operate at optimum capacity yet churn out unprofitable product. For example, "the Toyota problem," where on February, 23, 2010, Toyota acknowledged the inconvenience, death, and destruction its product caused.

Worthy of note: it is imperative that efficiency must not churn out a defective product as a result. A defective output results in a bad product. Besides, output is different from product. Output is a result of a manufacturing process of input that has gone through the process of throughput. But then, to create a product, you must factor in the economic value.

Product is the end of a full value chain proposition. It is what the consumer is willing and able to buy. Thus, in the creation of the product from your ideas, which comes through deliberate focus and investment on the faculties, you must factor in economic value.

Now, the brain is an efficient twenty-four-hour tireless machine that never goes to sleep. It has no idle moment or downtime, otherwise some of your critical neural coordinates would shut down, resulting in death. It is a fact that the brain processes every thought, especially your ideas. It is therefore important that you discipline your thought processes to create desirable products with economic value.

Important to note here is that for your ideas to have economic worth, you must factor in the consumer in the process. The questions therefore are: Is your idea bankable? Can you spend your hard-earned taxed income to purchase the product of your idea?

This reminds me of a life story involving the principal of a leading consulting firm in Nigeria. While in England, he conceptualized a particular unique type of furniture that took a lot of energy for the creation process. He almost went bankrupt using all he had to produce this special furniture. As far as he was concerned, it would be the best furniture the world has ever known.

The furniture never saw the light of day! He had abandoned every other thing and focused his entire energy and passion on the concept of this particular product. But then here comes a friend of his who asked him what he was up to. He tells his friend about this special furniture and how much it had taken him to conceptualize. Alas!

His friend asked a simple yet critical question: "Can you use your money to pay for this furniture if you are not its producer?" Moment of truth. It then occurred to the creator that he had embarked on a project whose product he wouldn't be willing to spend his money on. This, of course, meant the product was not bankable. He had not integrated or factored in the consumer in the ideation process of creating his special furniture. Painful as it may be, the project collapsed *ab initio*. That was a man who was sincere with himself. Many of us would have continued despite the obvious, and run into terrible loss and even indebtedness.

This illustration follows the Socratic saying, "Man, know thyself." It is not how good your business plan is that makes a good business idea. A business plan of a bad business idea is just what it is. Do not focus on the form but on the substance. There are many businesses that started without a business plan—for example, Microsoft. Once your idea is a good business idea and you consider critically your consumer in the processing of the idea into a veritable product or service, then you are good to go.

Note that just as it is important for you to do what you love, which is central to the sustainability of your personal energy required for the business, you must be interested in the problem of the consumer in order to be able to create a solution that meets his critical needs. *This implies that your solution must have neighborly application in deference to the injunction of the Holy Scripture:* "Love your neighbor as yourself" (Mark 12:31; Matthew 22:39). Your neighbor is not just the person living next door to you but the man or woman you meet at the critical crossroads of life. Indeed, your neighbor in this context is the potential consumer of your product. Man is born into troubles and problems; it is therefore your responsibility to deliver solutions to those innumerable problems.

Succinctly capturing this idea, the renowned French philosopher Jean Jack Rousseau says, "Man is born free but is everywhere in chains." It is important that in exploring your idle capacity, you develop bankable solutions for removing the chains, thereby creating demands that will bring you tremendous profit.

Besides, it is imperative that you define your unique competence and life philosophy. You must align your motions with the ideas of your brain. The fact that you don't know how your idea will work doesn't mean it's a bad idea. You can seek the help of a consultant or use self-help through deep study and meditation on the idea thoroughly.

It's important for you to note also that there is a difference between an idea and a notion. An idea has a developed work plan even when the idea is still hazy and unclear. A notion, on the other hand, has a careless tinge or coloration to it. Instead of a careless gist about your idea, you should develop a concept paper for it. You need to meditate through your idea and gradually flesh it out.

The questions that should concern you are

- What is your idea about?
- Under what circumstances can your idea be used?
- Who needs your idea?
- Why is your idea needed?
- Why would anyone want to pay for your idea?

You must realize that ideas do not understand the difference between day and night. They do not sleep. Therefore, you should cultivate a habit of putting a notebook beside your bed. Ideas are funny creatures. If you don't pay attention to them, they will move to the next guy. In fact, ideas sometimes take a life insurance policy on themselves by courting more than one person at a time.

A final note on this subject is that there are three parameters that govern the allocation of capital to an idea.

1) It demands high standards;
2) It does not abide carelessness; and
3) It does not condone error.

Therefore, you can't afford to idle away your ideas because an idea is basically a request for venture capital; non-ideas do not get capital, and bad ideas lose capital.

Thus, in following your ideas through from concept to reality, you must aim at a high standard, you must by necessary compulsion avoid carelessness, and you must create no room for error.

- Ideas are like Las Vegas casino chips, which are used in exchange for cash. And because ideas do not sleep, money never sleeps.
- Discipline yourself, and learn how to reach deep into yourself to grasp full utilization of the idle capacity in you.
- Be absolutely innovative and creative in the production of the object of your ideas.
- Create products the world would love to consume.
- Start and believe in yourself.
- Be fruitful and multiply your ideas.

CHAPTER 3

Developing Sustainable Creative Faculty for Business

T HE FOUNDATION OF any serious business is embedded in an idea birthed through the creative faculty. The following are the list of the brains behind the ideas that evolved into powerful corporations, some of which are Fortune 500 companies.

- Sam Walton (1918–92) invented the modern retailing system, opening huge stores offering discount prices in suburbs and rural areas that became economic anchors in those communities. The seed planted by this Arkansas businessman have today grown into Wal-Mart, the largest company in America as at 2010, with $422 billion in revenue and making $16 billion in profit in the same year.
- Alfred P. Sloan Jr. (1876–1966) not only built the General Motors (GM) behemoth but also created a corporate management system that was emulated for decades. GM introduced "a car for every purse and purpose," a strategy devised by the chairman to appeal to the emotional dimensions of the United States' mass market.

- Henry Ford (1863–1946) put the horseless carriage within reach of average families and thus created America's car culture. In 1908, Henry Ford introduced the Model T, which he called the car "for the great multitude, constructed of the best materials"—reliable, durable, and easy to fix. More than that, he revolutionized manufacturing with his assembly-line methods and was one of the first industry titans to understand the link between happy, satisfied workers and productivity. Ford Motors today is rated the tenth largest corporation in the United States with a revenue exceeding $128 billion and a profit exceeding $6 billion.

- Steve Wozniak (1950–) and Steve Jobs (1955–2011) rejected the assumption that computers should be confined to business use and would always take up huge amounts of space and cost. Their vision, which they help turn into reality through Apple, was to make the computer personal and place easy-to-use machines in the hands of average people. Their early efforts initiated the era of home computing, an establishment that is presently worth $65 billion in revenue, making $14 billion profit in the year in consideration, and also improving their ranking from fifty-sixth to thirty-fifth among the Fortune 500 companies. Besides, the company through the invention of iTunes have created new demands from customers who have continued to flock to it, creating a winning situation for recording companies and artists to the extent that they receive at least 65 percent of the purchase price of digitally downloaded songs. And as at today, iTunes Music Store now accounts for 70 percent of the legal music download market.

- Vera Ellen Wang (1949–) Daughter of affluent Chinese immigrants, Wang enjoyed a pampered childhood growing up on Manhattan's Upper East Side. A talented figure skater, Wang competed professionally throughout her teens. Upon her graduation from college, in 1971, Wang shelved her skating career and began working for Vogue magazine.

In 1987, she left Vogue to take a job as design director for accessories at Ralph Lauren. In 1989, frustrated with the slim selection of existing bridal wear, she sketched her own design and commissioned a dressmaker to tailor the elaborate gown at a cost of $10,000. The following year, with some financial backing from her father, Wang opened her own bridal boutique in the upscale Carlyle Hotel on Madison Avenue in New York City. Over the next few years, Wang honed her skills as a fashion designer and eventually launched a signature collection of streamlined and sophisticated bridal wear. By balancing modern designs with traditional elegance, Wang has acquired a large following, particularly in Hollywood.

- Sara Blakely (1971–) is one of the youngest self-made female billionaire who turned her life around with her idea of creating a new line of flattering undergarments. As the sole owner of her company 'Spanx' and net worth of over a billion dollars, Sara Blakely also reached the annual list of the 100 most influential people in the world by Time Magazine. The one-product wonder has now become the favorite of millions including almost all Hollywood actresses making 'Spanx' a billion dollar powerhouse. Its annual revenues reach 250 million dollars with Blakely never having to take any outside investment and any special marketing strategies.

- Akio Morita (1921–99) almost single-handedly changed the image of Japanese-made products in the United States and around the world—from cheap schlock to the highest quality. Morita and his Sony Corporation also triggered a consumer electronics revolution by making affordable but reliable products available to the mass market by offering innovations like the Sony Walkman: by looking across the high fidelity of boom boxes with the low price and mobility of transistor radios within the audio equipment industry, Morita's Sony created the personal portable-stereo in the late 1970s, drawing new customers like joggers and commuters into that market.

- Melinda Gates (1964–) Melinda Gates is co-chair of the Bill & Melinda Gates Foundation. Along with Bill Gates, she shapes and approves the foundation's strategies, reviews results, and sets the overall direction of the organization.
- Cher Wang (1958–) served as General Manager of PC Division at First International Computer Inc. Ms. Wang was a driving force behind First International Computer's (FIC) entry into the motherboard business. Her late father, Wang Yung-Ching, founded the Formosa Plastics Group, and was considered the second richest man in Taiwan before his death. She has both extensive experience and an enviable record in the electronics industry. She has been with First International Computer Inc. since 1980. Her remarkable insight into technology trends and entrepreneurship has enabled her to establish a number of highly successful IT-related businesses. She co-founded HTC Corp. in 1997. Ms. Wang has been the Chairman of the Board at HTC Corporation since June 20, 2007. She serves as the Acting Chairperson of High Tech Computer Corporation (HTC) and VIA Technologies and Chairman and Director of Everex Systems, Inc. In 2005, she was selected as an Innovator in the 2005 Stars of Asia: 25 Leaders on the Forefront of Change by Business Week and was named as one of the ten executives to watch in Asia
- William Hewlett (1913–2001) and David Packard (1912–96), with an investment of about $500, started their company in a garage. HP is now worth $126 billion in revenue and stands as the eleventh-largest corporation in America. Beginning with sound-testing equipment and later moving into computers, Hewlett and Packard built a global powerhouse years before anyone had heard of Silicon Valley or the PC, with HP profiting in 2010 to the tune of almost $9 billion.
- Oprah Winfrey (1954–) from her first job as a news anchor for a local TV station to an ailing daytime chat programme, The Oprah Winfrey Show started and has proved to be one

of the most successful and highly watched TV programme of all time. Oprah has also remained a powerful role model for women and black American women in particular. With earnings as high as $165 million between 2011 and 2012, Forbes opined rightly that she is one of the richest celebrities to have made their mark in the entertainment and cable TV network.

- Tyler Perry (1969–) Tyler Perry's inspirational journey from the hard streets of New Orleans to the heights of Hollywood's A-list is the stuff of American legend. Born into poverty and raised in a household scarred by abuse, Tyler took a simple piece of advice from Oprah Winfrey and sets his career in motion. After writing an inspired musical, *I Know I've Been Changed*, and in 1992, Tyler gathered his life's savings and set off for Atlanta in hopes of staging it for sold out crowds. In 1998 his perseverance paid off and a promoter booked the show for a limited run at a local church-turned-theatre. Soon the musical moved to Atlanta's prestigious Fox Theatre. Tyler has gone ahead to build an enviable business of over $78 million as at June 2013.

- Frederick Smith (1944–) wrote a term paper at Yale arguing for an overnight delivery service that would meet the need of a just-in-time economy and fill the lacuna created by the US postal monopoly. All he got in his term paper was a C, while he soon translated the substance of the ideas or thesis into Federal Express, which today delivers packages to more than two hundred countries in six hundred aircraft and forty-six thousand trucks.

- Andrea Jung (1959–) went from being a lackluster student to attending the Ivy League's Princeton University, and went on to become the CEO of Avon Products. Jung is the first female CEO at a cosmetics company who wasn't also its founder. Jung took the failing company out of the depths of marketing oblivion into a world of young, hip makeup products. When she started working for Avon Products, Inc., as a consultant in 1993, the company that had been around for over a hundred years was ailing, and needed a fresh burst of energy and life to keep it going. The higher-ups at Avon liked what Jung had to bring to the company as a consultant, and they hired her as president of the product marketing group for U.S. operations in 1994. In her first five years as CEO, Andrea Jung gave Avon a badly needed facelift. She is on the board of General Electric and was nominated to be on the board of the New York Stock Exchange. She is on the boards of such non-profit organizations as the New York Presbyterian Hospital and Catalyst, a company focused on women in business.

• J.K Rowling (1965–) As a single mother living in Edinburgh, Scotland, Rowling became an international literary sensation in 1999, when the first three installments of her Harry Potter children's book series took over the top three slots of The New York Times best-seller list after achieving similar success in her native United Kingdom. The phenomenal response to Rowling's books culminated in July 2000, when the fourth volume in the series, Harry Potter and the Goblet of Fire, became the fastest-selling book in history. Rowling, now Britain's 13th wealthiest woman, married anesthetist Dr. Neil Murray at the couple's home in Scotland in 2001.

It's germane that we understand that any genuine intention to build a sustainable business must first and foremost be grounded on a sustainable creative faculty fertile enough to produce ideas that could birth varying enterprises of one's choice. At this juncture, it's critical that we examine the power of our creative faculty and its limitless capacity, knowing full well that even though you cannot solve all problems in the world, there are some you probably have a firsthand experience of which can resolve by engaging your creative faculties. Every other thing will then depend on your ability to turn your problem-solving ideas into enterprise.

Suffice it to say the human brain, which is the cognitive processor of our creative faculty, has evolved over countless years, and the human being is like an information processing system with neurons extending to all our senses up to our very fingers and toes. And all these nerves send information back to the brain. Thus, our mind is a thought factory, and the factory produces thousands of thought each day. Therefore, it is important that we don't sell ourselves short nor take our creative faculty for granted because the result or product of our thought is the most basic ingredient for personal success in business and life in general.

According to Joan Minninger, in her book *Make Your Mind Work for You*, we have a committee with five major members called "the five minds." Imagine a boardroom with five members, and at the head is the CEO, or what we may call the "executive mind," who lays down rules, sets priorities, and gives orders, which could sometimes be fair, nurturing, and supportive but at other times domineering. It could sometimes inspire the other minds to cooperate and sometimes incite them to rebel. It arbitrates among the other minds, and without it we can't make decisions. This faculty is given prominence in many execution-oriented leaders who often have to follow through on the people-centric process, the strategy, and the operating plan in order to get things done in organizations. It's key to the success of leaders who are involved in rigorously discussing the hows and whats, questioning and tenaciously following through, and ensuring accountability. Such leaders make informed assumptions about a business environment, assess the organization's capabilities, link strategy to operations and the people who would implement the strategy, synchronize those people and their various disciplines, and link rewards to outcomes. Moreover, they coordinate the flow of the mechanisms for changing assumptions as the environment changes and upgrade the company's capabilities to meet the challenges of an ambitious strategy.

There is also the "organizing mind," which is the part of us that analyses and sorts, without which we cannot think rationally or see things clearly or get the job done. This faculty adores the rules dished out by the "executive mind" and helps the executive mind follow through on actions. It looks carefully at every situation and gives a realistic approach to things and weighs the pros and cons of every situation we face, keeping our mind as clear as possible within many options available to us.

There is also the "reacting mind," which responds to stimuli with emotions and feelings. Without this faculty we wouldn't be alive, nor would we have any motivation to do anything. It helps us realize that our reactions—that is, our immediate feelings or emotions—are good indicators of what we really want or desire and we should value them. It's imperative to know that it's natural to feel all our emotions one time or the other, as long as they don't dominate our lives, and can be channeled to positive and productive action when possible. (That is why leaders must have the emotional fortitude to get things done.)

With the benefit of hindsight, the forty-second president of the United States, Bill Clinton, with the help of his reacting mind, he was always able to empathize easily with the American people and their plight, and that won him a second term, aside the fact that he explores his ability to balance a budget, even when he was at the brink of being impeached over a sex scandal with an intern, Monica Lewinski.

There is also the "knowing mind," which collects data from the senses and processes it into information, without which we would dwell in a sensory and informational void. It simply expedites and conveys information. It works effectively in allowing the executive mind to direct it correctly and coherently.

And then we have the "wondering mind," which represents our creative faculty, that part of us that is curious, inventive, experimental, and playful, and without which we'd lack creativity, would not be able to solve problems, and would be unable to deal with new and unfamiliar situation. It is therefore imperative that our "executive mind" lay out the guidelines for our wandering mind while we allow it a lot of freedom, allow it break new ground, and give it freedom to think of new ideas and approaches. We should let our creative faculty have fun; we should enjoy our creativity and our imagination and all the things that makes us special, because it's this enjoyment that makes life worthwhile. And when we give our creative faculty confidence, we are bound to produce amazing things. We should encourage our creative faculty to think big, to think successfully, and to believe in ourselves. Our ability to properly coordinate the various faculties of our mind is the lasting elixir for success in business and life.

We must have plans for personal success and learn how to overcome the enemies of success such as fear, excuses, self doubt, procrastination and so on. We must learn effective confidence-building techniques such as the vacuum analysis technique discussed about, and learn how to turn defeat and setbacks into victories. We must discover how to make our attitudes our ally for achieving success. We must know how to think and act like a leader. Success is a goal of life, and the size of our success can only be limited by the size of our thinking and by extension to the extent to which we allow our creative faculty to operate. If we think small with small ideas, with small ambition, then our success, in turn, will be small; but if we think big and believe in ourselves and encourage our creative faculty to extend beyond boundaries and reach out with "blue ocean" innovations and ideas, our success will also be big.

We have to train our creative faculty to believe big and be ambitious. Our capacity and ability to develop a sustainable creative faculty has a lot to do with our ability to believe big and think great ideas. Belief is like a thermostat that regulates what we accomplish in life. A man who believes very little receives very little and accomplishes very little, because the lack of belief in himself will reveal through the way he walks, talks, reads, and goes about his enterprise. Unless he can readjust his belief thermostat forward, he's going to continue shrinking; and since others see in us what we see in ourselves, he'll grow smaller in the estimation of the people around him.

Oftentimes we observe that an upwardly mobile person believes he's worth a great deal, unpalatable circumstances notwithstanding, and in a matter of time, he receives a great deal. He believes he can handle big, important, and difficult assignment and, through this, makes a massive impact anywhere he finds himself. The strength of belief often boosts the capacity for use of our creative faculty or imagination, as it has been said that man can create anything he can imagine.

History abounds with lessons that through the development and use of the creative faculty, man was able to discover and harness nature's forces more in the last fifty years than during the entire history of the human race previous to that time. Today, we travel in jet airlines because two bicycle mechanics, Orville and Wilbur Wright, believed in themselves and developed their creative faculties. Man has analyzed and weighed the sun at a distance of millions of miles, unraveling through the aid of the creative faculty the elements of which the sun consists. Man has increased the speed of locomotion such that today he can travel at almost unimaginable speeds. The creative faculty, or what has been referred to as the faculty of creative imagination, is the communication link between the finite mind and the infinite intelligence. It is the faculty through which hunches and inspirations are received. It is by this faculty that all basic or new ideas are handed over.

This creative faculty functions only when the conscious mind is working at an exceedingly rapid rate, such as when it is stimulated through the emotions of a strong desire. Indeed the creative faculty becomes more alert in proportion to its development through use. The great leaders of business, industry, finance, and the great artists, musicians, poets, and writers became great because they developed, in a consistent and sustainable manner, the faculty of their creative imagination and thus have made and are still making a massive impact on the world today.

Besides, there is no end to one's productivity once limitations to man's creative potential have been lifted. Indeed, corporations all over the world that operate on a sustainable platform of creative engagement often witness product improvement, technological transformation, and self-renewing models of operation. As a result of this, some have triggered positive change in the industry in which they operate. Thus, you either improve your ideas and the way you drive the engine room of your organization or you perish by declaring bankruptcy or bear the risk of being acquired by a rival company.

For example, following is the story of how the famous Coca-Cola brand came to be. Several years ago, an old country doctor drove to town, went into a drug store, and had a long but quiet conversation with the young clerk. After a while, the doctor returned with a large, old-fashioned kettle and a big wooden paddle (used for stirring the contents of the kettle) and deposited them at the back of the store. The young clerk inspected the kettle and paid for it with his entire savings. The doctor then handed over a small slip of paper containing a secret formula, which is today worth a king's ransom. Yet little did the two know they had just initiated the beginning of an empire that would stand as one of the world's best-known brands.

What began by a seemingly insignificant transaction between the doctor and the drug clerk has paid and still pays huge sums of money to men and women all over the world. The same old "kettle" is one of the world's largest consumers of sugar, thus providing jobs to thousands of men and women engaged in growing sugarcane and in refining and marketing sugar. It also consumes, annually, millions of glass bottle, providing jobs to a huge member of glass workers. It gives employment to an army of clerks, copywriters, and brand and advertising experts throughout the world. It has brought fame and fortune to scores of artists, who have created magnificent pictures describing the product. The influence and impact of the idea has today become of tremendous benefit to every civilized country in the world.

As of today, Coca-Cola uses 350 billion gallons of water for its product per year. It has more than a thousand factories in two hundred markets worldwide, yet CEO Muhtar Kent has set another vision to keep the brand above the competition regardless of its hitherto success. In an interview with Sarah Green in the *Harvard Business Review*, Kent stated he set a ten-year plan that will double the size of the company. He believes that between now and 2020, they can achieve what they have not achieved in all their years of existence as a corporation, by creating a roadmap for winning, creating transformation, building a stronger brand, continually cracking the codes of growth, and improving the company's brand matrix.

This company has existed for more than a century and believes there are no limits to the development of sustainable ideas, keeping the company consistently above the cutthroat competition.

Now, some corporations, owing to the complexity of doing business in these modern times, have chosen to be more cognitive in their approach by consistently creating diverse platforms to thrive in the development and use of their creative faculties in an uncontested market space. This is one strategic way of making a difference with an idea by creating a company that builds a future where customers, employees, shareholders, and society win. Instead of dividing existing and often-shrinking demands and benchmarking competitors, you develop an execution-oriented strategy tailored toward growing demand and break away from the competition, making the competition irrelevant. This is maximizing opportunity while minimizing risk. This is blue ocean strategy.

A strategic example would be Guy Laliberte, a one-time accordion player who turned an almost-moribund company into one of Canada's largest cultural exports. Cirque du Soleil was created in 1984 by Guy Laliberté and Gilles Ste-Croix and their group of street performers in the midst of a declining, no-longer-attractive industry in which traditional strategic analysis pointed to limited potential for growth. The global champion of the circus industry, as a result of various alternative forms of entertainment (besides children preferring PlayStations to a visit to the traveling circus), were experiencing steadily decreasing audiences, leading to declining revenue and profits.

Instead of Cirque du Soleil having to compete with the industry champions, Ringling Bros. and Barnum & Bailey, who set the standards for the industry, or competing with smaller circuses, it created an entirely new market space that made the competition irrelevant. As a result, its productions attracted a new viewership and have been seen, since 1984, by almost one hundred million people in more than 271 cities on every continent except Antarctica. In fewer than twenty years, Cirque du Soleil was able to achieve a level of revenue that took the industry leader more than one hundred years to attain, thanks to superior ideas and sustained platforms of creative thinking. It accomplished this by appealing to a whole new group of customers, adults, and corporate clients prepared to pay a price several times as great as a traditional circus for an unprecedented entertainment experience.

According to Korean-born business theorist W. Chan Kim,

> At the time of its debut, other circuses focused on benchmarking one another and maximizing their share of already-shrinking demand by tweaking traditional circus act. This included trying to secure more famous clowns and lion tamers, a strategy that raised circuses' cost structure without substantially altering the circus experience. The result was rising costs without rising revenues, and a downward spiral of overall circus demand.

Cirque du Soleil demarcated itself from this traditional structure, style, and logic of the circus and created a totally new experience that made the competition irrelevant. It intelligently worked away from the economies of the traditional circus that only yielded low revenue and increased cost structure.

W. Chan Kim further maintains:

> By injecting the concept of multiple productions and by giving people a reason to come to the circus more frequently, Cirque du Soleil has dramatically increased demand. In short, Cirque du Soleil offers the best of both circus and theater, and it has eliminated or reduced everything else. By offering unprecedented utility, Cirque

du Soleil has created a "blue ocean" and has invented a new form of live entertainment, one that is markedly different from both traditional circus and theater. At the same time, by eliminating many of the most costly elements of the circus, it has dramatically reduced its cost structure, achieving both differentiation and low cost.

This is an apt example of a company that developed, through engaging the creative faculty, a well-executed blue-ocean strategy with a profitable business model. Another case in point is the tremendous success of Southwest Airlines, a corporation in Dallas, Texas, becoming a Fortune 500 company in 2010 with a revenue of $12 billion and a profit of $459 million. They achieved their remarkable success by offering, through value innovation, high speed transport with frequent and flexible departures at prices attractive to the mass market, something that was not common within the airline industry. According to W. Chan Kim,

> By eliminating and reducing certain factors of competition and raising others in the traditional airline industry, as well as by creating new factors drawn from the alternative industry of car transport, Southwest Airlines was able to offer unprecedented utility for air travelers and achieve a leap in value with a low-cost business model.

This has made their assets increase to more than fifteen billion dollars. Incredible! This is an attestation to dedication and consistent execution of a profitable business model through the "blue-ocean strategy," which challenges companies to break out of the "red ocean of bloody competition" by creating uncontested market space that makes the competition irrelevant.

CHAPTER 4

Developing the Spirit
of Creative Entrepreneurship

MY USE OF the words creative entrepreneurship were carefully considered and applied to suit the purpose intended here. It is critical that as a director in a company that has hitherto operated as a small business for about five years but at the moment is being reengineered to become a full-blown corporation, you pay close attention to the thoughts developed in this chapter. Also, in establishing a formidable management with competence in investment analysis, banking, and capital market, it's noteworthy to mention that the words creative entrepreneurship have not been carelessly applied here and were definitely not used as a "beer-parlor" business-philosophy.

As an example, I offer the innocent excitement my baby boy exudes as he grows day by day. He is now one year old, and I cannot help but marvel at his enthusiasm. I was privileged to watch him at close range at home for a month, and I concluded that this is creativity even from the cradle. He will do nothing but cry when you hinder him from going about his adventures. One day he went to the book shelf and dragged out some books I had yet to study, including *Blue Ocean Strategy* by W. Chan Kim and *Execution* by Larry Bossidy, books that were critical to mine. He pulled out any available box and pursued my laptop, phones, and any other gadget in sight, often trying to jump from the bed to reach any object of his fancy, not considering the possibility of falling, never afraid of failing at a mission or project of his fancy. He starts afresh on a new day as if a new dawn has come with different challenges, hopes, and aspirations with keen interest on any task he engages in. He often smiles in excitement, forgives in an instant, and moves on, approaching every moment with fresh vigor.

Suffice it to say, in today's world you either explore or exploit your creative ability in your chosen enterprise, or you perish. It takes a lot for companies to remain on the top of their corporate position, and many are dying by the day, one of many implications being an increase in unemployment. In this connection, instead of moving closer to accomplishing the millennium development goals, most developing countries are drifting farther from it. It is not just enough to go into business; you have to make your departure crystal clear from the standpoint of creative entrepreneurship.

Around one million people in the United States start a business every year, but within the first five years, about 80 percent (eight hundred thousand) of those will have failed. By the end of the second five years, another 40 percent would be out of business. There is no hiding place for most emerging economies. Many businesses go into chaos and become unmanageable and unprofitable, not because they don't work, but because they are established on a flawed foundation. This is by far the biggest reason for the failure of many small businesses today. The panacea is for us to consistently develop our capacity for creative entrepreneurship.

The absolute need for people and businesses to continue to improve their capacity for inventiveness and creative entrepreneurship derives from current realities, which have seen the world growing inexorably into a more and more competitive place. For example, consider *Forbes* magazine's list in 1917 of the one hundred most powerful corporations. By 1987, seventy years later, sixty-one companies had died and thirty-nine still existed, and out of these thirty-nine, only eighteen had managed to remain at the top of the list of one hundred best companies. This remaining eighteen had underperformed in the stock market by 20 percent, and only two—Kodak and General Electric—outperformed the market within this seventy-year period. But now Kodak is gone, and only GE remains, and it took the genius of their CEO, Jack Welch, to bring GE from a $13 billion organization to a $494 billion cash cow within the twenty years of his reign.

For obvious reasons, we will briefly consider Welch's seven winning ways, many of which remain great lessons today and reveal him as a product of creative entrepreneurship.

1. Welch instituted an aggressive program of buying and selling, acquiring and discarding businesses predicated on the realities of changing consumer tastes, the economic and political environment, and the relative strength of the competition.

2. Welch reduced excessive costs and cut corporate fat through restructuring and downsizing and by extension responded to the painful process that corporate America had to go through in the 1980s to be able to swim rather than sink in the red ocean of bloody competition in the global economy. The implication was that he was able to prove his emotional fortitude in his first twelve years as GE leader as he downsized the employee base from some 440,000 to just more than 200,000, which he later build up again to 313,000. Though a painful action that only a pragmatic and an execution-oriented leader can afford, it did set the stage for the longest period of economic expansion in the history of the United States (*Jack Welch and Leadership 2001*).

3. Welch turned GE into a post-industrial company where manufacturing, while still vital, took a back seat in favor of services. He made a well-calculated, highly proactive response to the undeniable reality of the transition from America's shrinking manufacturing sector to a services- and information-based economy, through which he built a company that drew 70 percent of its revenue from services.

4. Welch placed an intense focus on shareholder value, product quality, and customer service. Through initiatives such as the Six Sigma program, GE was able to avoid the reputation for shoddy products and poor services that afflicted many companies in the United States and as a result was able to consistently execute record investment to the company, notwithstanding the economic downturn and a bloody, competitive environment.

5. Welch transformed GE into a truly global company. While GE had pursued overseas markets for some eighty years, Welch accelerated the company's integration into the rapidly globalizing economy of the 1980s and '90s, taking the share of revenues generated from global operations from less than 20 percent to well over 40 percent during his tenure as CEO. And with 95 percent of the world's population living outside US borders, many of them in exploding markets like China's, Welch's emphasis on globalization has proven well-placed.

6. Welch embraced a culture of change and spread it throughout GE, making the company more nimble and less bureaucratic while others like it slid toward extinction. While insisting, with emotional fortitude and leadership tenacity, that GE as a company should not only embrace change consistently, it should operate with the soul of a small company while being a big company, Welch got rid of businesses (even those with high sentimental value like housewares) to buying NBC and embracing the Internet.

7. Welch created a company that became a magnet for human talent, empowered this talent, and transformed employees into leaders and committed stakeholders in GE's success. Through training, mentoring, freewheeling exchanges, and a carefully calibrated system of "carrots and sticks," he was able to accomplish the aforesaid, giving rise to peak performance while massively improving the company's productivity and competitiveness. Welch laid bare the reality of the

claim of most CEOs, that people are the company's most valuable asset. Alongside this courageous moves was Welch's passionate, execution-oriented, emotionally balanced, and highly cognitive leadership, which made GE a place where people wanted to be, a place where things were happening, a place where people's hunger to be part of a course beyond themselves could be well nourished.

Without a doubt, these actions, courageous as they might be, are replicable by the leadership of any organization that would be ready to get committed.

We deem it imperative to enquire further into GE's legacy of success and innovation by making reference to the time of its founder, Thomas A. Edison, as recorded by James W. Robinson.

- 1879: Edison invents the carbon filament incandescent lamp. The first commercially practical lamp lasts forty hours.
- 1880: Further innovations by Edison extend his lamp's life to six hundred hours. The first lamp factory is opened in Menlo Park, New Jersey.
- 1896: A GE engineer builds electrical equipment for the production of X-rays and demonstrates their use in diagnosing bone fractures.
- 1900: GE opens the first industry laboratory for scientific research in Schenectady, New York.
- 1902: A GE consulting engineer patents the electric fan.
- 1903: GE installs the largest steam turbine yet developed, a five thousand-kilowatt unit in Chicago.
- 1905: GE's first electric toaster hits the market.
- 1906: The world's first radio broadcast is accomplished by a GE engineer after he developed the high-frequency alternator that made radio broadcasts possible.
- 1908: GE develops and supplies electric locomotives for the New York Central Railroad.

- 1910: GE makes the first Hotpoint electric range.
- 1912: GE builds the first electrically propelled US Navy ship, *The Jupiter*.
- 1914: GE designs the electrically controlled locks for the Panama Canal.
- 1915: The safety of electric stoves is significantly enhanced with GE's development of a ceramic insulation called Calrod.
- 1918: GE develops a new alternator that makes possible the first transoceanic radio communication. Also, a new GE vacuum tube is invented that later became a key component in radar systems and microwave ovens.
- 1921: GE's Sanford Moss develops the supercharger that paves the way for high-speed, high-altitude airline flight.
- 1922: GE opens radio station WGY in Schenectady, one of the first to transmit regular broadcasts.
- 1927: GE inaugurates the first TV reception in a home in Schenectady.
- 1929: GE installs a new power generator unit in Indiana, with a capacity four times greater than current models.
- 1930: GE puts the first electric washing machine in the market. The company also establishes its plastic division.
- 1932: The GE Credit Corporation is created to finance consumer purchases of the company's growing array of home appliances.
- 1935: New high-powered lamps from GE made possible the first nighttime major league baseball game in Cincinnati, Ohio.
- 1940: WRGB in Schenectady, owned by GE, becomes the first station to relay broadcasts from New York City, laying the groundwork for the first television network.
- 1941: GE builds America's first jet engine.
- 1943: GE engineers invent the first airplane autopilot device.
- 1945: GE introduces the first commercial use of radar.
- 1947: Hotpoint, a GE brand, markets the first cooking equipment for fast-food restaurants.

- 1955: GE develops the process for manufacturing man-made diamonds, setting the stage for a new generation of industrial tools and machinery.
- 1956: Newly developed GE engines power the Convair Skylark, the first commercially viable jet plane. The company also establishes its management-training center in Crotonville, New York.
- 1962: A GE scientist invents the solid state laser, paving the way for the development of such products as the compact disc player and the laser printer.
- 1978: GE builds the world's largest nuclear power plant in Japan.
- 1981: The revolution in fiber-optic communications is spurred by GE components that make possible twenty-five-mile-long fiber-optic strands.
- 1986: New US car models are introduced that contain a record amount of GE plastics as a substitute material for many components. 1991: GE passes IBM as the most highly valued company in America.
- 1992: GE builds the Mars Observer for NASA.
- 1994: GE becomes the first Fortune 500 company outside the computer industry to go online.
- 1999: GE Medical Systems introduces a new imaging technology that allows doctors and surgeons see the clearest picture yet of diseases within the human body.

It is important that we take into consideration the fact that we live in an age of never-satisfied-customers, and if you take into account the responsiveness of a company like Amazon.com or e-Bay, you will demand the best from whomever you're doing business with. Creative entrepreneurship does not begin with the picture of the business to be created but with the customer for whom the business intended.

The creative entrepreneur clearly understands that the business is the product, and the customer is always an opportunity. He knows that within the customer is a continuous array of changing wants begging to be satisfied. It is for this reason that GE, under Jack Welch, rather than fizzle out of existence like other giant corporations that had impressive histories of scientific inventions and revolutionary development, it consistently committed itself to innovations through massive expenditures on research and development, sometime to the tune of $2.2 billion annually (James W. Robinson 2001), while buying and selling an array of businesses. It established businesses engaged in aviation services, commercial equipment financing, and commercial finance. Other businesses it established include Employers Reinsurance Corporation (ERC); Financial Assurance; GE Equity, which is a subsidiary of GE Capital; Mortgage Insurance Corporation; and NBC, which also owns thirteen television stations and operates MSNBC with Microsoft, real estate, structured finance group, transportation systems, vendor financial services, and others like it, making the image of the old electric lightbulb company remain frozen somewhere in the hazy past.

It is in this light that the turn-key revolution (a type of project constructed so it could be sold to any buyer as a completed product) massively impacted and still impacts small businesses in America, transforming them from a condition of chaos into order, excitement, and continuous growth. It was this revolution that ultimately birthed a business model that works, the franchise phenomenon, made popular by McDonald's Ray Kroc.

At age fifty-two Ray Kroc, with only 36 percent of his productive life remaining (according to David J. Schwartz [*The Magic of Thinking Big* 1959], most people are expected to have fifty years of productive life from about ages twenty to seventy), he created the most successful small business in the world. In McDonald's, customers know they will get the same type of food, prepared the same way, whether they visit a McDonald's in Moscow or Minneapolis. Costumers feel confident in McDonald's, and as a result, a new McDonald's location has a head start on success compared to an independent hamburger stand.

How do you perceive opportunities when you see them? Do you merely observe them as a spectator, or do you unleash the sparks of your imagination as a creative entrepreneur while making full use of the opportunity around you?

Ray Kroc saw things in a different light. Soon after his visit, and having been possessed by a passion he had never felt before, he convinced the hamburger stand brothers to permit him to franchise their method. Within twelve years he bought them out and went on to create the largest retail prepared-food distribution system in the world, indeed the most successful small business in the world. The success of McDonald's is truly staggering, such that in fewer than forty years, Ray Kroc's McDonald's has become a $40 billion a year business, with 28,707 restaurant worldwide and growing every minute, serving food to more than 43 million people every day in 120 countries all over the world. The average McDonald's restaurant was producing more than $2 million on annual sales, and it was more profitable than any other retail business in the world, with an average of 17 percent pretax net profit. Ray Kroc through his creative entrepreneurship capability created much more than a fantastically successful business—he created a model upon which an entire generation of entrepreneurs have since made their fortune, a model that formed the genesis of the franchise phenomenon.

For the purpose of those who cared to grow beyond their comfort zone, to enlarge their capacity for creative entrepreneurship, it become necessary to take a peek into records made available by Michael E. Gerber, who noted in his book *eMyth Revisited: Why Most Small Businesses Don't Work and What to Do about It* (1985) that the success of the McDonald's franchise model started in trickles. In consequence, some entrepreneurs began to experiment with Ray Kroc's formula for success. *And since the year 2000, there have been 320,000 franchising businesses in 75 industries.* Franchising produces $1 trillion dollars in sales each year in the United States alone, almost 50 percent of every retail dollar spent in the nation, and had more than eight million foreign part-time people—the largest employer of high school youths in the economy of the United States.

But then the genius of McDonald's is not in franchising. Franchising has been around for more than ten decades. Many giant corporations such as Coca-Cola and General Motors have utilized franchising as an effective method of distribution to broadly and inexpensively expand their market. Besides, the true genius of McDonald's is in the business format franchise. The early franchise businesses, many of which still exist, were called "trade-name franchises." Under this system, the franchiser licenses the right to small companies to market its nationally known product locally. But the business-format franchise took a step beyond this by not only lending its name to smaller enterprises but providing the franchisee with an entire system of doing business.

This type of franchise maintains a belief that runs contrary to what most business founders believe, which is that the success of the business resides in the success of the products. Yet the business-format franchise is anchored on the belief that the true product of the business is not what it sells but how it sells it. The true product of the business is the business itself. Thus, Ray Kroc understood that rather than hamburger being the product, McDonald's was indeed the product.

But Ray Kroc was a consummate entrepreneur, and like most entrepreneurs, he suffered a major setback: he had a huge dream but very little money. The franchisee thus became the vehicle for him to realize his dream. At this point, he began to look at the business as his product and the franchisee as his first, last, and most important customer, for this franchisee was not interested in hamburgers but in the business.

Driven by the desire to buy a business, the franchisee was interested in one question: Does it work? Ray Kroc's most important concern then became how to make sure his business worked better than any other—if McDonalds was to fulfill the dream he had for it, the franchisee would have to be willing to buy it, and the only way to ensure this was for Ray Kroc to make sure McDonald's worked better than any other business opportunity around. The second reason was that given the failure rate of most small businesses, he must have realized that for McDonald to be a predictable success, the business would have to work. Once Ray Kroc understood this, his problem became his opportunity: first, creating a business that worked in order to sell it; second, creating a business that worked once it was sold regardless of who bought it.

Armed with this realization, Ray Kroc started out the task of creating a foolproof, predictable business, a systems-dependant, not people-dependant business, a business that could work without him. Ray Kroc thus went to work on rather than in his business. He thought about his business like an engineer working on a preproduction prototype of a mass producible product. He brought to bear his genius of creative entrepreneurship in thinking about McDonald's like Henry Ford must have explored the production of the Model T: how the component of the prototype could be constructed so it could be assembled at a very low cost with totally interchangeable parts. How could the components be constructed so that the resultant business system could be replicated over and over again, each business working as reliably as the thousands that preceded it?

What Ray Kroc did was to apply the thinking behind the Industrial Revolution in the most creative manner to the process of business development and to a degree never before experienced in a business enterprise. The business as a product would only sell if it worked, and the only way to make certain it works in the hands of a franchisee anywhere in the world would be to build it out of perfectly predictable components that could be tested in a prototype long before ever going into mass production.

Oftentimes what has been found within corporations that started with tremendous success but later crumbled is an arrogance that comes with success, seeing it as an entitlement rather than following the apostle Paul's dictum of forgetting the past and looking forward to the future. Therefore, to succeed as a creative entrepreneur, we must operate a careful, strategic "forgetful management" style Otherwise it would have been impossible for Jack Welch to put the successes and highly impressive legacies of GE behind him and break the code of growth for the company.

This is the same path the CEO of Coca-Cola is set to toe now. His resolve to double the size of Coca-Cola within ten years looks like madness and indeed appears reaching beyond the possible, an attempt that could lead to the decline of Coca-Cola. But then, being a resourceful entrepreneur that he is, while adhering to highly disciplined management practices, he does not appear to be making a merely bold but untested strategy but seems to be pursuing a path of disciplined creativity informed by a scientific approach toward management based on informed data.

In his interview with Sarah Green, when asked why he has chosen the United States to be his center of focus to execute his proposed ten-year vision of success for Coca-Cola, he revealed that the United States is a growing demographic and will add thirty million people to its more than three hundred million population in ten years. It is also a diverse and an entrepreneurial population that receives half of all skilled people that emigrate around the world and that, by implication, is a tremendous influx of skilled labor. Besides, the United States has an innovative population with more than 60 percent of patents registered in the world; couple this with the fact that in the next ten years, demographics claims there will be about a billion people who will reach middle–class status worldwide, and you will have another eight hundred million people urbanized, the biggest urbanization the world has ever known. This means a city the size of New York will be created all over the world in the next ten years.

Arguably though, these are stupendous, pragmatic, scientific facts that the creative entrepreneur can exploit for a big transformation, informed by penetrating understanding and insight that tends to avoid the hubris that makes giant corporations depart into insignificance and irrelevance, as instructed by Jim Collins (*How The Mighty Fall* 2009).

Nonetheless, it is noteworthy that one of the safety nets for sustainable creative entrepreneurship is to outright avoid undisciplined actions such as unchecked and unrestrained leaps into arenas for which you have no burning passion; taking action inconsistent with your core values; investing capital and creative energy in new arenas where you cannot attain distinctive capability that is superior to that of your competitor; launching headlong into activities that do not fit with your economic or resource engine; ignoring blue-ocean strategic approaches; and neglecting your core business area while leaping after exciting new ventures. It is indeed counterproductive to abandon or relegate to the background the primordial values of your vision, mission, and focus or to use the organization primarily as a vehicle to increase your own personal success—more wealth, more fame, more power. We are, in this connection, instructed by Packard's law (an insight inspired by David Packard, cofounder of HP), which states "No company can consistently grow revenues faster than its ability to get enough of the right people to implement that growth and still become a great company. [And] if a company consistently grows revenue faster than its ability to get enough of the right people to implement that growth, it will not simply stagnate; it will fall."

It follows then that the primary question is not which product, concept, or strategy to engage in to drive success in the business but who to drive the business toward. The concern is first about getting the right people on the platform of your business enterprise: people who are self-managed and self-motivated; people who will naturally work with you to promote a culture of discipline because they are disciplined themselves, highly talented individuals who consistently think outside the box; people who are not afraid to engage in a productive, robust argument on executing whatever strategy that will bring growth and deliver the desired revenue for the company; people who will naturally grow to become the best managers in the industry and could eventually be recruited as CEOs of other companies; people who are resourceful entrepreneurs themselves, who will be flexible enough to accommodate your creative entrepreneurial drive. The number-one job of creative entrepreneurial leaders is the recruitment, nurturing, development, and retention of awesome talent. In other words, the leader's job is to find, develop, manage, and deploy talent for the values and purpose of the company, besides adequately paying the talent.

DISSOLVING THE COMPLEXITIES IN BUSINESS ENTERPRISE THROUGH CREATIVE ENTREPRENEURSHIP

It has been proven that business enterprises are more than ever becoming increasingly complex, defying predominant rules of operations. Business enterprises, just like ideas, are taking life assurance on themselves rather than thrusting themselves in anybody's arms. Major solutions that are being proffered to these myriads of complex problems are as plentiful as the solution volunteers wearing the "Kantian spectacles," where time and space, Kant says, are irremovable spectacles through which we view the world. Wearing the Kantian spectacles is like a man wearing blue glasses—everything he sees will be appear blue even though they really aren't. Hence, the way things appear to that man would be different from the way they really are. This leads us to the distinction between noumena—things as they really are, and phenomena—things as they appear to us.

The implication is that our minds therefore impose their own structure on things, forcing the things we perceive to conform to the internal structure of the percipient. In other words, our mind imposes its own categories on objects or the problem we perceive, and it forces them to conform to these categories during the cognitive process. Attempts to solve the problems are articulated within the realm of cause and effect.

A cause is that which something (an effect) is produced. We consider categories such as quantity, unity, plurality, totality, quality, reality, negation and limitation, relation and modality, and so on, yet we do not know what's going on. Thus things have become more complicated, especially in the twenty-first century, and the problems of business enterprises have refused to make themselves amenable to tidy mathematics. Despite people's best intentions, the ultimate result, such as the global recession, has proven unanticipated.

Don't even imagine that because you are a nice person (cool, calm, and collected) nothing bad will happen to you. For instance, despite the fact the United States is the most generous nation in the world ($300 billion is donated by the United States per annum, which is greater than the GDP of many nations in Africa), this has not endeared the United States to all nations of the world. Everybody's problem is America's problem, but America's problem is obviously only America's problem!

It is the same with business enterprise all over the world. It is even worse in the various unstable economies in Africa. Besides, in this system we do not know how things will unfold, as the problems of business enterprises continue to daily refuse to yield to experts' predictions. It is also obvious the solution that we seek may not possibly be extracted from experts. This clearly is the task the creative entrepreneur is set to tackle. Our stream of imaginative creation will have to be laid bare through constructive congregation of diverse groups of highly talented, intelligent people.

The number-one responsibility of a creative entrepreneur and his executive group, who are interested in clinically dissolving enterprise complexity, is to hire highly talented, creative, and diverse people. This is because when there is an aggregation of intelligent, hardworking, and talented people with different training, experiences, and personalities operating under a system of cognitive diversity, we are bound to have a hotbed of creativity. This is fundamental to achieving significant success in any enterprise, simply because in a cognitively diverse environment, people are rigorous and creative enough to accommodate robust and execution-oriented thinking; they will offer different points of view that would challenge one another and also challenge the status quo within the organization; they will go beyond talking about only the organization's shared information and bring to bear unique private information (that they would have ordinarily reserved to themselves). And where there are healthy incentives for diverse information generation and aggregation, creative answers to enterprise problems may be readily obtained.

Indeed, it is the well-coordinated interaction of the diverse group of people in the organization that will bring about extraordinary execution of projects and strategy in the organization.

Most of the time, aside from the fact that our natural inclination is to hang out with people who are mostly like us (people with whom we think and talk like and probably attended school with, most organizations), rather than recruit people with high intellectual curiosity with different skills, experiences, and exposures, companies would constitute the executive cadre in such a way as to be made up of people who mostly are "yes men" instead of those who are bold enough to give them frank assessment of the state of affairs at every particular moment in the organization. As a result, the leaders are not able to effectively access the information in people's heads. They are not able to extract the unshared information from everybody in order to lay it bare for proper evaluation and engagement.

When these leaders gather for their executive meetings, the first subject of discourse is usually not about hiring the right people or how to nurture, develop, and retain them and get the wrong ones out, but they focus on budget, strategy, financial analysis, and so on. They quickly forget that even great corporate vision—without highly intelligent, emotionally balanced, hardworking, execution-oriented whiz kids to drive the vision—may run into irrelevance and extinction over the long haul.

The first thing to do is to hire enough talent in order to create enough excitement: intelligent, proactive, pragmatic and execution-oriented people. Creative entrepreneurs would first figure out who should get on the bus before considering where to drive that bus. When there is an urgent need to create an extraordinary momentum that would further drive the organization, the task of getting the right people on the bus (and the wrong people out) is highly imperative. The authentic creative entrepreneur believes that if the right people are brought along, enough excitement would be created through a well-coordinated and robust cognitive process that would bring to life the momentum that would eventually lead to sustainable high performance and fulfillment of organizational vision. This is because such people have the required mental alertness to accommodate complex issues and engage in robust arguments and at the same time have fun, while dealing with the challenge of future change.

It is my belief that this formed the basis of the success of Jack Welch during his reign as CEO of GE. But then, he had dealt with the number-one issue, which was to create an enabling environment for high performers, for the right people to operate the "GE bus," getting rid of the wrong people in the company (to the tune of 240,000 employees during his first twelve years as CEO), while building it up again with 113,000 more of the right people. In this way, Jack Welch was able to develop formidable managers who became the envy of the corporate world; employees who were loyal to the company's determination to total overhauling and rethinking of enterprise strategy, who believed him, who engaged him in robust argument. Once a decision was made, everybody was sure about what to do. And those right people were able to help him execute the extraordinary projects of GE that brought them such massive fortune, which by May 2001 stood at $498.64 billion. With Welsh, they established the company as numero uno in the corporate world.

Let us turn our attention to the consistent successes of one of the giants in the world, a corporation that occupies, as at 2013, the twenty-fifth position on the Fortune 500, and indeed one of the biggest banks in America, Wells Fargo. Out of Wells Fargo's more than ten million retail customers, a third (about four million) bank online. Yet their online customers have stayed with the bank longer and probably remained happier, with 99 percent of those customers not having met anybody from Wells Fargo. This clearly reveals bold steps toward creative entrepreneurship and a total corporate innovativeness. This would not have been possible if Wells Fargo did not focus on injecting an endless stream of talents directly into the veins of the company, employing and integrating massive technology that changed the world's view of banking, recruiting outstanding people whenever and wherever they found them.

Dick Cooley, the CEO who launched Wells Fargo into this platform of imaginativeness, got the best people available, built a strong team of partners, highly diverse personalities who ferociously debated eyeball-to-eyeball in search for the best answers, building them into the best managers in the industry. And the company is still going strong despite the stormy weather of global recession in the corporate world, which has led to the collapse of many giant corporations, leaving several others at the mercy of government bail-out plans.

When leaders of corporations bring in the right people, an executive team of rivals who are creative and highly resourceful entrepreneurs in their own right; people who will not blindly agree by default to authority; people who are self-driven and talented; people who have built their own platform into the very best yet still have the humility as well as emotional fortitude and sense of responsibility to meld their own strengths with others' in order to execute whatever strategy it would take to make a company successful, there is nothing that can possibly stop such an organization from occupying the zenith for a long time. The leaders should not bore such people with their own points of view, coming into a meeting with ready answers while expecting them to just rubber-stamp their views. The leaders should step back while creating the healthy platform for an organization of diverse views to surface, allowing the unique unshared information to come to the table for clinical evaluation while making sure no particular voice overshadows or dominates others. Everybody should be given a free hand to make contributions.

And when the leaders have devised an effective means of extracting the information through robust interaction, in the most practical and pragmatic process and within the fundamental rules of engagement; when a decision is arrived at and it's clear what each person should do to execute his or her own part of the decision made or strategy devised for accomplishing an extraordinary project, the intended dynamics would easily be achievable and the company would seamlessly snowball into greatness, making a massive impact nationally and globally.

CHAPTER 5

Advancing Enterprise through Social Capital and Networking

M ORE THAN A century ago, Charles Darwin proposed that empathy, the prelude to compassionate action, has been a powerful aid to survival in nature's toolkit.

Six rhesus monkeys were trained to pull chains to get food. At one point a seventh monkey, in full view of the others, got a painful shock whenever one pulled the chain for food. On seeing the pain of that shocked monkey, four of the original rhesus monkeys start pulling a different chain, one that delivered less food but inflicted no shock. The fifth monkey stopped pulling any chain at all for five days, and the sixth for twelve days—that is, they starved themselves to prevent shocking the seventh monkey. In furtherance of this account, and according to author, psychologist, and science journalist Daniel Goleman, "Empathy lubricates sociability, and we humans are the social animal per excellence ... our sociability has been the primary survival strategy of primate species, including our own." It is on this premise we desire to and explore in this work the content, the human potential for social capital and social networks the engagement of which would be germane to the expansion and promotion of business enterprise in a sustainable way.

There is a tendency in humans to collaborate rather than compete among themselves. This happens even at the subliminal level of the psyche but is triggered to the surface upon provocation. This is fundamental to the development of our communal nature as a people, especially as Africans. We easily empathize with each other, which makes us inclined to protect the territory of our friends, sometimes at our own expense. Could it be traceable to the fact that "human brains have vast tracts of well-proven neural architecture in common with other mammals, especially primates," (Goleman 2006) and that, "the similarities across species in sympathetic distress, coupled with the impulse to help, strongly suggests a like set of underlying circuitry in the brain"? Or are we merely following the bandwagon simply because others are?

Social capital is a concept that refers to connection within and between social networks, which highlights the value of social relations and the role of cooperation and confidence in accomplishing collective or economic result. In other words, it is the fruit of social relations and consists of expectative benefits derived from the preferential treatment and cooperation between individuals and groups. This implies the relevance and value of social networks and, by extension, its capacity to affect the productivity of individuals and groups. The questions here are: How have you been able to explore your goodwill, fellowship, and mutual sympathy, social intercourse among your group, to count and be relevant in the daily running of your enterprise? And how have you improved your performance through the functionality of your strategic alliances and enhanced supply-chain relations?

A typical example is that of a colleague of my wife's, who works in a bank. This young man has expanded to boost his network among the creative class in Nigeria: actors, actresses, musicians in different genres, comedians, and so forth. Being a banker, he often participates in their concerns by helping them facilitate short-term loans through his personal portfolio and that of other friends and colleagues in the bank with whom he has developed trust over the years. For instance, one of his friends is a reputable comedian who had traveled abroad. He learned this comedian's wife urgently needed cash to deal with some domestic issues back home. All he did was contact our banker friend, who approached the situation without hesitation, facilitated the securing of a short-term loan with which the wife was able to sort herself out without having her husband cut short his trip. This friend records little or no default because he often deals with reputable individuals of various professional calling. And they amply appreciate him for always coming to their aid, knowing fully well that the cost of getting cash in the country is rather expensive. As a result, he often gets invitation to their events, be it the premier of a movie, musical concert, or show, any event at all. He is regarded as one of the most sociable banker in the country at the moment because he's often seen around at events of all sorts, and more so, he meets far beyond his target, as a business development person or a marketer if you like, in the bank. He has switched from one bank to another several times without his popularity dwindling. Indeed, his popularity keeps increasing.

The young banker described in the illustration above has put to use social capital and networking to further improve and strengthened his career prospects, since most of his friends keep their account with him. Hence, most bank CEOs want him on their team because he easily brings tremendous economic value to the organization.

A family made a five-day trip to Brazil, and on getting there, being an unfamiliar terrain, they kept to themselves. Their reserved manners had closed them off from the disposition of the Brazilians as the family were too preoccupied as to respond to the friendliness of the Brazilian. But as they relaxed and began to pay close attention to those around them, it was as though they zeroed in on the right station, the warmth that was there *ab initio*. They soon noticed that the people they met seemed friendlier by the day, experiencing greater warmth and rapport.

Oftentimes, because of our own uptightness and personal inhibitions, we are reserved and often appear unfriendly even in a warm and friendly atmosphere; we are unable to experience the enhanced power that comes with increased personal access and skills that could come through social networks; and we expunge ourselves from the cooperation and mutual support that social capital facilitates.

A close friend of mine, who was a senior manager in a transnational bank in the country, was able to make tremendous success as a banker through his resolve to utilize to full advantage his social networks. He moved from being an executive assistant to about three successive CEOs in the bank to becoming a business development manager and then manager of branches that were not performing in terms of financial targets, and went on to becoming the head of public sector, a new department that was created specifically for him to bring in more deposits to the bank, moving him from one country to another in Africa. My friend has a genius for moving into the midst of any gathering of people to socially network them, to make friends with them, and before long he gets their account at the bank. And by this, he has been able to rake billions of naira into the bank. He has thus been awarded with cash benefits. He often frees himself at the very start from any kind of inhibition that may hinder him from utilizing his social contacts.

Besides, social capital cannot be depleted by use but in fact by non-use. So our friend, from getting long- and short-term loans for his customers and members of his social networks at good interest rates moved to depositing their money in fix accounts and getting them the best interest rate they could ever get. Who wouldn't want to deal with such a banker who creates a win-win situation for both his clients and the organization?

Again, social capital could refer to the collective value of all social networks and the inclinations that arise from these networks to do things for each other. It is indeed an investment in social relations with expected returns in the marketplace. It's imperative to note that it is an investment before returns are accruable to us if we are going to benefit from the interactions we engage in. *You must consistently seek the good of your social networks, and it must be obvious that you are bringing something to the table. Your social unit must be able to profit from some particular information you have access to and some of your skills that could either improve their own skills or improve their lifestyle or make life easier for them.* This makes them have warm disposition toward you and has the capacity to make them release themselves to your cause at the time you need it most.

Actions that are prompted by cognitive energy as a result of social capital often start with you appearing in someone's radius of perception: "I notice you, I feel for you, so I will help you." This implies that you often cannot tell the extent of help you could get from your social networks by appearing consistently in their view or registering your presence before them. You could make yourself available to their struggle through volunteer work of any kind or a coordinated and intelligent gathering of information and other resources that could be of great assistance in the acquisition of skills and traits valued in the marketplace (such as tips about job vacancies, access to credit, etc.). And when you bring a product to them for purchase as a solution to their need, they can easily feel with you since you have made an impact. By implication you have invested time and energy—cognitive and emotional. They tend, therefore, to take note of you as someone who has their interest at heart, so they act to help you by purchasing your product, making referrals on your behalf to others, linking you to other webs of social connects that you perhaps had no idea about, using their influence in any capacity to bring you economic gains.

The government of the Federal Republic of Nigeria withdrew subsidy on petrol early January 2012 pursuant to the policy of deregulation of the downstream sector of the oil and gas industry. As a result, the pump price of gas went up from 65 naira to about 145 naira, which led to a mass protest by Nigerians. Several social groups formed a network for massive peaceful protest all over the country for a week. Civil society groups; labor unions; the creative class consisting of musicians and entertainers of different genres; comedians; marketplace men and women; representatives of professional bodies;

and students and other youth groups were all inspired by a common cause that the gas price must return to the original price. As the protest proceeded day after day, various groups exploited the social capital the occasion afforded as the network became increasingly widened. Each using virtual media provided mutual feedback through Facebook, Twitter, a BlackBerry network, and so on.

The country was technically shut down for a whole week, accounting for unimaginable economic loss both to the public and private sectors. As a result, the federal government initiated the call for negotiation with the leadership of the labor unions.

The point is that mustering the mass protest couldn't have been possible without the network of various social groups convinced about their cause. The mass action was effective in twisting the hand of the government on account of nothing other than social capital and networking. This indeed reveals the power of social networking as a tool for driving and influencing change in a nation. Consider the spread of protests started December 18, 2010, in the Arab nations, termed "The Arab Spring."

Listening to someone tell an unhappy story in doleful tones activates the listener's motor cortex, which guides movements, as well as the amygdala (an almond-shaped area in the midbrain, the trigger point for many emotional reactions) and related circuits for sadness. For instance, I would like you to consider the story about the painful experience of my family in respect of my wife's journey to conception and motherhood. She tells her own story hence.

"My Journey from Infertility to Motherhood"
Dolapo Taiwo-Fajolu

In the Beginning

Getting married was high on my priority list once I survived the long and arduous journey to achieving academic qualification. By the time I was through with school and landed a plum job in the bank, there was nothing stopping me and my fiancé from taking the plunge. We were ready and believed in our dreams of starting a family immediately.

At thirty-one, I couldn't wait to start making babies. I didn't feel anything could stop me from getting pregnant on the first try. I was healthy, and had a clock-work regular cycle. Also, no one in my family had to deal with infertility, so I felt it would be a breeze. Although, a few years prior, I had discovered milky-like discharges from my left breast and went for a checkup after following which I told my mum. The doctor said it was probably nothing to be worried about as there were no lumps. I had no idea that that "nothing" was actually a major sign of an abnormality that would delay my attempts at conceiving.

GETTING WORRIED

After Eight months of unprotected, deliberate sex and no pregnancy, I began to worry that something was wrong. My hubby didn't see any problem and would jokingly ask me what the rush was for? I began to suspect the discharges from my breast were something more than nothing especially as it now leaked from both breasts. I Googled it and what I discovered was frightening.

MY DIAGNOSIS: PROLACTIN AND INFERTILITY

It was from medical journals and Googled articles that I discovered a world of prolactin levels and infertility. I went to a specialist hospital armed with the information I already had about my condition and the blood work revealed a higher than normal level of prolactin. The doctor confirmed that my periods, though regular were just my uterus shedding its walls.

The shock of the news, the fear of treatment, and all the associated psychological issues were overwhelming.

Another term for high prolactin levels is hyperprolactinemia. Women who are not pregnant and are not breastfeeding should have low levels of prolactin. While Prolactin plays a vital role during lactation and breast development in pregnancy, If a non-pregnant woman has abnormally high levels of prolactin, it may cause her difficulty in becoming pregnant. The occurrence of a milky flow from the breast of a woman who has not recently been pregnant or nursing is called galactorrhea. This was the initial condition I experienced that the doctor I visited did not see anything to worry about! While galactorrhea can be caused by excessive local stimulation as well as hormonal imbalance, a full examination to rule out the cause should have occurred.

The doctor had to eliminate the causes of my galactorrhea. Some medications cause an increase in prolactin levels. One of such was a drug I was using for ulcer (Cimetidine). Other drugs that could result in galactorrhea include some types of antidepressants, sedatives, estrogen, oral contraceptives (birth control pills), blood pressure medications (methyldopa, verapamil), and medication for nausea (Reglan, metoclopramide). It can sometimes also be due to physical stress.

I was placed on a high course of Bromocriptine (Parlodel) and six weeks into treatment, I conceived! *Oh,* I thought, *if I only knew it was that simple!* But then I miscarried. This happened twice and then nothing again for months. The doctor placed me on a regime of weekly injections to boost my hormones and I got pregnant again. This third time, the pregnancy went past the first trimester and into the twenty-fourth week, but all of a sudden I began to dilate and my cervix couldn't hold up again!

By the time I got to the hospital that fateful first Saturday in January 2009, I was twenty-four weeks into my pregnancy and four centimeters dilated. The doctor told us the prognosis was bad; my baby's lungs were immature and could risk grave infections if born at that age. He did an emergency cerclage. Cervical cerclage is a rarely used type of surgery that involves sewing shut the outlet of the uterus (cervix) to prevent it from opening before a pregnancy is carried to full term.

I was placed on full bed rest, and we began to pray for a miracle. The doctor opined that if I could keep my son in for four to six more weeks, he would have a high chance of survival. I must add that the cases of premature births in Nigeria are very high and most hospitals are not equipped for the care of such delicate children. Three days into my bed rest, my water broke and I had to deliver my son prematurely. He didn't survive the delivery and died immediately after. The devastation I felt was indescribable. It was just five days into a new year, and I could not believe I was starting it on such a sour note.

The diagnosis was clear—my cervix gave up midway into my pregnancy. The doctor said the condition is not predetermined and most times, it is diagnosed only when it has happened. Now apart from hyperprolactinemia, I had to contend with an incompetent cervix! I felt my world crashing on me and was depressed for a long time. Friends and family came around and in a few months I was ready to begin the journey again. Now this time, with the Parlodel, the injections, and all, I was finding it difficult to repeat the magic that made me conceive before. And how could I forget the crazy side effects of Parlodel? I constantly felt sorry for myself, and sex with my husband was more of a reproductive research than an expression of love.

I went through several procedures: HSG (X-ray examination of the uterus, fallopian tubes, and surrounding areas); laparoscopy; D&C to remove tissue in the uterus after the miscarriage; you name it. I felt violated, invaded, and oftentimes just sick of all the probing and needles.

I am a believer, and my husband and I serve God as workers in our church. We prayed for God to step in. We took communion together daily, and around that time we listened to Pastor Poju Oyemade of Covenant Christian Center in Lagos talk about the power of confession. We wrote our confessions and consistently declared that we were parents of the kind of children we wanted. About that time we changed churches to a place that was instrumental in developing our faith beyond serving God to relating with God as a powerful and miracle-working Father.

I had peace that God would give me children, I just didn't know when. I still took my drugs the entire time. I knew I had to get pregnant! Do you know what it feels like when all the women around you are either pregnant or have a baby? Apart from the emotional and physical issues, there is also the societal stigma that is prevalent in our Naija society. People ask, how many children do you have now? Those who know you are still waiting are careful not to upset you, and at the same time, you really want to rejoice with your friends who are having children, but deep down you feel sad about your condition.

The same society that places a high mark on fertility, however, lacks the moral and spiritual guidance and counseling backing needed to help people face these challenges.

Medical counseling is rare if not nonexistent, and most doctors are seeing the high infertility rate in the country solely from an entrepreneurial point of view rather than a balance of providing succor and solution to a prevalent problem.

In June 2010 I realized I was late. I took a pregnancy test and it was positive. I didn't know how to react as elation was mixed with fear, but I was determined to do all the right things for this child. So with prayers and the best medical care available, I proceeded with my pregnancy. I researched my condition and took note of all my symptoms. This pregnancy from the beginning was unlike any I'd had before. I was sick and experienced bleeding at the eighth and eleventh weeks. I had cervical cerclage when I was at thirteen weeks. Now all I had to do was take things easy, take my medications, and lie low. The months moved slowly, and every week that passed brought relief. I was constantly in pain and sometimes felt like my pelvis would burst, but prayers and faith in God's words and my confession kept me going.

When I passed the twenty-four-week mark, I celebrated quietly as my pregnancy had passed the point where I'd lost my last baby. However, at thirty weeks, I began to lose my mucous plug and then started having discharges of mucous and blood. By now I was on complete bed rest, and the doctor was hoping I could carry my son beyond thirty-two weeks.

That was not to be as my water broke early one beautiful Monday morning. The cervical stitches were removed, and I delivered my son, who weighed 3.5 pounds, and we immediately began the Neonatal Intensive Care Unit (NICU) ordeal.

Prior to this I had never met or spoken to anyone who had a preterm baby, and all the experiences I read about online were different from my Nigerian situation.

I was, however, consoled that my son and I received the best treatment a Nigerian hospital can offer and from a plummeting weight loss of 3 pounds, he gradually began to gain weight. After four weeks in the NICU, at 3.5 pounds, and having overcome apnea and luckily escaping jaundice (a miracle I praise God for), I took my son home.

I learned some valuable lessons while in the hospital, one of which is that you are your own counselor and encourager. Another lesson is that no matter how hard you worry, God is in control, and he has your best interest at hand.

MOVING FORWARD

There are women who have fertility issues that have gone undiagnosed or been misdiagnosed. Many today spend a lot of money on tests that are either too expensive or invasive or outright unnecessary.

So many women are hiding away because of the stigma ascribed to infertility in our society, and many groan under the persecution and label of barrenness. There are hardly counselors or teachers who are willing to show the way, and where biology has failed, spiritual lessons are one-sided or insufficient. Even the Bible says a barren womb is unsatisfied! As long as the woman is not with child, there can never be fulfillment! How then can we help? How can knowledge empower us? How can we be sure our circumstances will not be exploited by entrepreneurs in our money-driven society? I advise women to arm themselves with knowledge, to be brave, and to face their illnesses or whatever is causing delay.

The first step toward healing is acceptance. Accept you have a problem, identify your symptoms, if any, and check your diet. Most delays can be from our partners as well, so the test should include semen analysis. A good doctor will not start to treat you without first confirming the status of your spouse's semen. Lifestyle changes too are key to finding healing. Apart from this, there is the belief that external influence beyond the physical causes infertility. I would be fooling myself if I didn't mention this, as our African roots and society are riddled with such stories of people being cursed or placed under the influence of juju or voodoo. While not glorifying the Devil, who is masterful in deceit, it is important to note that the Almighty God is sovereign and more powerful than any influence. So I hold the belief that no voodoo, charm, or juju is able to keep a woman barren. Once your faith is in gear, believe the Word of God concerning your situation, learn all you can about it, and keep believing. Once that is done, other steps follow.

I also would like to candidly advise that as women, we should not wait too late to begin child-bearing if interested in having children and the opportunity presents itself. As much as we can, and is possible, we should start early. Yes, I know the economic situation and relationship problems may cause delays, but we must encourage the young ones to start early, especially if motherhood is a high priority in life. It is a known fact that the older a woman becomes the harder it is to get pregnant, and there are associated complications/age-related defects that might arise with the pregnancy despite current technological advances.

*

Without a doubt, this was a painful story to tell, although it ended on a happy note. It's not the kind of narrative to be made public considering the cultural conservation among our people and despite the fact that the issue is not only real to many but prevalent in our society. Yet people prefer to keep it to themselves for the reasons of either stigmatization or ignorance. Thus, the first time it was published in a blog, the narrator got about two hundred responses the first day, and many more afterward. Many were able to relate to her story and applauded her courage. Later, a member of her social network who empathized with the story and felt the need to publish it on a larger platform asked our permission to publish it in one of the reputable national dailies. It would later appear as a full two-page story, which ordinarily could have cost us a whopping five hundred thousand naira. We've also been able to help other families within our social networks deal with similar challenge by providing them with valuable information that has helped them go through the process, reducing the burden of fear of stigmatization and empowering them to make courageous decisions.

The impact of this moving story has snowballed into partnership with an NGO geared toward making provision of facilities needed for care of premature babies in the ICUs of private and public hospitals.

Besides, it's not how robust our balance sheet is that is crucial in life, even though adequate capital is highly imperative for business as a going concern. Thus, the concept of social capital helps us in no small measure to explore the social network platform in full advantage, be it a small business or a giant corporation or any enterprise at all.

For instance, a friend who resigned his bank position as a senior manager to start his own business with some foreign partners was able to utilize his social networks platform to secure, in fewer than three month, a funding line to the tune of N1.5 billion from one of Nigeria's foremost banks. This will in no small way advance whatever business his partners and he intend to engage in, all things being equal. Thus they'll be able to contribute their quota in creating employment opportunities and actively participate in the economic growth of the country.

The use of the Internet has proven to have positive effects on social capital. The rapid growth of social networking sites such as Facebook and Twitter is a positive indication that individuals are developing their virtual-network platform. Unlike face-to-face interactions, people can instantly connect with others in a targeted fashion by placing specific parameters with Internet use. This means massive opportunity is now available for individuals to selectively connect with others based on ascertained interests and backgrounds.

Of course, on a larger scale, social capital is also the aggregate of the actual or potential resources, which are linked to possession of a durable network of more or less institutionalized relationships of mutual acquaintance or recognition. It has been used as a veritable tool to orchestrate sustainable growth for one of Europe's largest banks to the extent that while the world's economy was in recession, and the global financial industry was grappling with issues of legitimacy, this bank was extending its footprint with superior value with the regulators and customers, increasing its overall lending by 13 percent, its mortgage lending by 21 percent, and its loans to small- and medium-sized businesses by 14 percent.

They achieved this success by first developing a distinctive business model with a clear strategy on how to execute it, while everyone faithfully stuck with it. With tremendous focus, every employee became bound by this determination to look beyond his particular unit or part to doing the right thing for the bank and the clients, striving to generate high performance in creating long-term economic value, producing significant benefits for the wider community, and building robust social capital within the organization.

The leadership of the bank was committed to drawing on an expansive view of the company's heritage and cultural, organizational, and social assets. They built the widespread commitment as well as capabilities to execute the model by developing the organization into a community of shared purpose, marked by high level of emotional connection, trust, and respect, and this they did over the long term. As they repositioned the company by increasing trust and commitment, the leaders created a higher-energy, lower-friction organization that has an improved capacity to execute and deliver greater economic value. Also, they extended the robustness of the social capital within the network of staff of the organization as well as improved social value outside the organization, generating further economic value and inspiring the organization to greater heights.

The bank refocused its attention strategically on Asia, Africa, and the Middle East, the emerging economies where the bank had institutional history, deep local knowledge and interactions, and robust social relationships, where it had competitive advantage. The bank has a carefully documented vision with a strong strategic framework to be the best international bank by global reach with a profound social capital capacity and a deep local knowledge that would make it possible for it to be "a right partner" for its customers.

The bank's leadership made sure to strengthen the role of the country's CEOs and build trust among local shareholders. And as far as they were concerned, it takes more than incentives to make a complex matrix structure work; the social connect and relationship is crucial— in fact, the social actors here must be ready to create and mobilize their network connections within and between the organization to gain access to other social actors' resources, and people must feel comfortable working directly with others outside traditional lines of command. Decisions wouldn't get bumped up the hierarchy, and everybody had a clear understanding of the decisions made and the direction the organization was going, thereby increasing the capacity for projects and strategy to be executed; everybody onboard had to be able to appreciate diverse opinions, working styles, and national cultures and build and improve the social connects within a company that are strong enough to transcend those differences. As they got people to work in different dimension of the matrix, the less biased and "strait jacketed" they become, the more diverse they became for authentic and genuine transformation. And thus, they insist that the managers be effective collaborators, a skill they were being coached on and supported with, on which they would personally be evaluated.

Needless to say that, there is perception of "a common evil" among CEOs and managers of giant corporations, a problem of a personality disorder that makes them believe they know everything—and of course the truth is, they don't. Especially in this part of the world where many of them, rather than get sacked for an incompetent management of their most formidable asset, the people, the talents at their disposal get pampered by the board that they often manipulate until a shakeup is brought about by a radical change. This was occasioned by the intervention of regulatory agencies witnessed in the financial sector in Nigeria around 2006, where the number of banks in the country shrank to about twenty-five. This was also witnessed in the shakeup of the board and management of the Nigerian Stock Exchange (NSE), the Security and Exchange Commission (SEC), and others. We also witness this as some of our most formidable financial institutions in Europe and America declare bankruptcy despite previous massive mergers or acquisitions, which many were made to believe would shore up solvency for the affected organizations.

As far as Leif Johansson, the CEO of Volvo, is concerned, there is the need for leaders of corporations and business enterprise in general to create a connect between economic and social values of their organization by creating a superior employment experience for every employee. Organizations should focus consistently on building a community of shared purposes through shared values, strong emotional attachment, and high levels of mutual trust and respect across the strata of the organization. This has helped it to operate at elevated levels long enough to increase the capacity of the company's vision to take root and come to fruition. Besides, operating through the models of social capital makes an organization strong within and across all its local markets. And for this reason, the CEO crafted his strategy and execution plan around a steady and deliberate focus on Volvo's need as a social institution.

Johansson strongly holds the view that the key to achieving his goals for the company, which was just picking up the pieces from the failure of former chairman and CEO Pehr G. Gyllenhammar, is to reinforce people's emotional attachment to the company and to build much higher levels of trust and mutual respect. He is convinced there would be need for social connects of people of different tongues and nations, of different experiences and functions, working together for the first time in a wholly new way, if Volvo is to be strongly established as a global powerhouse. And having suffered badly from what he claims was the critical weakness in the Volvo culture, the hubris—an arrogance and complacency about its own professionalism that had contributed to a poor track record as a company—he went on to delineate the values of the company with words like "energy" and "passion" as articulated in the company's guiding document, addressing culture, values, and the desired behavior, which are now used in the recruiting process, performance evaluation, and by extension promotion decision throughout the Volvo group. And indeed, mutual respect must accord a company an extended capacity to take advantage of diversity and productively resolve conflicts.

When the value of mutual respect is deeply engrained in the culture of an organization, no matter how diverse—in terms of different tongues, people, and nationality, exposure, experience, and function—there would be a high level of ability to engage in robust argument within a controlled system, with nobody taking any issue personally as the overall objective is to build a superior structure that makes the company advance in its enterprise. Hitherto, social capital, for Volvo, has become a culture that makes it progress with new acquisitions.

For all intents and purposes, the nation-building enterprise and the capacity of nations, especially emerging economies, to experience an authentic sociopolitical and economic sustainability should be anchored on a clearly delineated concept of social capital. Social capital as a concept could thus be applicable to organizations and associations (including public, private, and nonprofit). It holds the social fiber tightly together and thus lowers the cost of doing business and as well increases productivity by promoting trust, coordination, and cooperation within every strata of the society. And there is increasing evidence that proves social capital is a fundamental tool that functions critically for the growth of economies, just as it is indeed highly relevant to the advancement of the human enterprise since it helps spread prosperity among the people.

CHAPTER 6

Accelerating Performance of Business Enterprise through Modern Technology Devices

N OWADAYS, BUSINESS ENTERPRISES are driven by technology since it helps generate the next great economic idea. Most businesses now use, at the very least, a PC or desktop, modem or cable connection, the Internet, and printers. They are used to keeping customer records electronically and are better able to find ways to serve the needs of their current and future customers. Companies can outsource customer service, order lines, or even programming and technology, saving between 30 and 70 percent of in-house costs. The e-mail and Internet have shrunk the world such that businesses of all sizes can attract global customers. In addition, the efficiency of order entry, inventory control, and supply-chain integration make it more cost-effective to do business in many areas. We should not forget marketing—databases keep track of customer desires, past purchases, and even what customers look at on a website. Algorithms can then generate lists of similar or ancillary products and services, creating a more robust experience and relationship with the client (Wilson 1999).

Global business, the bread and butter of several of today's emerging enterprises, brings executives into head-to-head contact with other executives of diverse cultural backgrounds. It has become obvious that individuals of different cultures have issues communicating efficiently than they do with those from identical cultures. Intense international rivalry constricts profit margins as well, and market settings are changing so rapidly that there is hardly ever time for a second chance at a mismanaged contract negotiation due to some kind of miscommunication. Consequently, international business communication becomes a challenging and important responsibility for those executives who are paving the way for progression into international markets (Limsamarnphun 2011).

Modern technology has significantly hastened the rate at which we can create letters, documents, notes, and voice communications, but these obsolete workflow examples are incompetent arteries of businesses with terabytes of hard-to-find information.

The consequential strain causes individuals to reach for technological remedies that might alleviate departmental congestion but eventually does little to holistically develop business performance and might even damage it in certain ways.

When talking about wide performance improvement, a main human strength is aerobic competence. Likewise no matter how intricate a gas engine is, it is at its core just an enormous air pump, and flow and throughput are key to improving power output.

If we see the modern business with its countless organs and constituents as a human body, then information flow is equivalent to the blood and oxygen supply. People in the past believed anything could be accomplished by taking control of the things into our hands. Certainly there will be some temporary disruption from time to time. Nevertheless, in today's environment, there is no easy way out. As soon as a change is assimilated, another one pops up (Killer 1996). Generally there are countless changes taking place altogether. There is limited control over the environment, and in order to navigate through these rapid times, caution should be exercised. Vision and leadership make thriving change. As the change agent, the first step is to craft a vision of the future that is able to focus on the group's energy (Kemp et al. 1996). The vision should contrast what is with what could be and should be inclusive enough to guide how the gap of the future should be abridged.

Information technology (IT) is a broad term that includes a combination of the acquisition, processing, storage, and dissemination of information in a computing or telecommunications platform. In terms of a scientific discipline it is relatively new, appearing in a 1958 article in the *Harvard Business Review* in which the authors said, "This new technology does not yet have a single established name. We shall call it information technology (IT)" (Dunn 2011). The field has been part of the tremendous growth in computing and telecommunications and remains vital—it is behind the recent emergence of next generation web technology, bio information, cloud computing, global-information systems, and large-scale databases. Present-day information era has given lots of freedom to the citizens, which was not probable without the arrival of this age. The users of information systems have available information, for example, the full *Encyclopedia Britannica* on one CD, with all types of search features available, pointing toward correct information within the right time. Picture doing this with the book version of the encyclopedia, sieving through several pages while looking out for the information alphabetically and still not being able to retrieve it.

Another benefit of information systems is the accessibility of real-time information on any area. For example, users can log in to their banks' website, credit card site, or share markets for any online transaction. No doubt this provides convenience, but it also comes with its own price of managing the security of the transactions. Crimes against information systems is a growing concern amongst cyber security experts and federal law enforcement agencies as this has the potential to bring down a system and operation that otherwise would run smoothly.

Many scholars see the greatest single influence on the changes in the practice of medicine since World War II to be the development of technology. Database technology allows doctors to handle complex information (patient records, test results, X-rays, and other tests) and share this data with specialists around the world. Doctors no longer need to be physically located in the same room as the patient to view and review their case. In addition, information can travel with the patient throughout their lives, making it far easier to see patterns. Educationally, IT helps doctors practice to be doctors without needing as much dissection—virtual programs assist in learning surgery, anatomy, and complex organic chemical reactions. Advances in computer memory and technology also allow for quicker development of X-rays and scans, as well as quicker blood and urine test results. Finally, technology, particularly biotechnology, has a huge effect on disease prevention and, through gene therapy, diseases that were once incurable are now easier to manage (Gupta 2005).

The complexity of health-care has snowballed over the years, and it has become increasingly probable that practitioners would not be fully notified about patients' current and previous health status and treatment. The use of modern information technologies, such as the accessibility of powerful computers and continually developing software, new high-speed networks, and economical massive storage capability, together with the extraordinary growth in Internet and intranet usage, have led to a rise in the quantity and accessibility of electronic health information.

Availability of pertinent data presents incredible perspectives such as supporting health-care professionals in their everyday tasks and research work, decreasing clinical errors, and consequently amplifying the quality of health-care. Electronic medical records (EMRs) are an electronic patient health-care record with complete interoperability within an enterprise. EMRs are designed on unique software connected in a networked setting between various departments within a health-care setting. One of the most significant benefits of EMRs is the convenience of information. Looking for medical information in the EMR is easy and prompt. Since the information is uploaded on a server that is connected to several networks, any person can access the information from any designated and authorized network. Moreover, the quality of information is excellent since there are hardly any missing pieces of data in the EMR.

Even though the health-care sector is eager to take full advantage of the EMR, it should be realized that implementing EMRs in individual organizations is not a solution to all its issues (Ethier 2002). In fact, EMR implementation will provide an opportunity to reexamine and restructure the organization's operational processes, clinical workflows, paperwork, structure, policies, and training programs.

New technologies will encourage the expansion of numerous innovative applications, shifting the lifestyle of billions in terms of communication, conduction of business, and intermingling with machines. Groundbreaking technologies of the future, united with satellite growth and artificial intelligence, will open a surplus of new business models and new prospects for the future.

CHAPTER 7

The Critical Launch Pad for Nigeria: an Economic Imperative

I N THIS CHAPTER, we shall focus attention on the African market, especially Nigeria, being the largest black nation in the world. In this regard, the two fundamental questions of sociopolitical theory, namely, "who gets what?" and "says who?" shall engage our interest for resolution. One bothers on the distribution of material goods, and of rights and liberties—on what basis should the citizens of a country possess property? And what rights and liberties should they enjoy? The other question, however, attempts to grapple with the concern of distribution of political power. Political power in this context refers to the capacity and the right to command others, and to subject them to sanctions if they disobey.

Any cognitive energy unleashed on this terrain of thought will lead to an emergence of ideas that could delineate the sociopolitical economy of the people, engaging one with issues that highlights Nigeria as a clinical example of a nation-state and also as a nation that should have a massive economic relevance to the continent. This is in respect to her potential in the establishment of institutions that have the capacity to protect the property rights of the people and set control through consistent policies that would create a formidable platform for creative entrepreneurs to thrive, more so, as a complex adaptive system. In my opinion, these are fundamental rationales that would create a massive launch-pad for Nigeria to experience genuine and sustainable economic development.

This gives credence to the Aristotelian claim that man is a rational being, and in the process of exercising his rationality to the fullest, he erects structures that enable him to maximize these potentials. Yet society is structured in a manner that makes absolute freedom impossible. A person's right to freedom of movement for instance is inhibited by another's right to privacy. One's right to freedom of expression is limited by another's right to a good reputation, or the former's freedom, if uncontrolled, could impinge on the latter's other fundamental rights.

The fundamental concerns in concert with the foregoing is the reason government as an institution of state is established as the sum total of the agencies by which a state is governed for the actualization of its objectives. It is the agency through which the will of the state is formulated, expressed, and realized. And while society is an association of human beings and suggests the whole complex of the relations of man to his fellows, consisting of the complicated network of groups and institutions expressing human association, the state as one of the groups, and indeed, the most important of the group, is a way of regulating human conduct, which is basically concerned with those social relationships that express themselves through government. Yet a nation is an agglomeration of people of common descent, language, history, etc. inhabiting a territory bounded by defined limits. On this note, Nigeria could be referred to as a nation state.

Now, as a nation state, it became imperative for Nigeria that the government and national institutions focus on public policy, which favors impersonal contracts between strangers in an economic market, and formal controls to enforce them. Of course, society exists and is strengthened by some instruments and institutions, both natural and manmade, that regulates man's behavior. Life would be anarchic and property made unsafe in the absence of institutions.

In fact, modern economic growth did not proceed until the institutions of capitalism, which emerged for the purpose of securing private property rights, freedom of contracts, and the rule of law, capital accumulation, innovation, and industrial enterprise, ushering in an extraordinary and sustained rise in living standards. Besides, these institutions of capitalism—private property rights, free contracts, and the rule of law—have in a major way made all the difference between misery and prosperity among nations of the world. And that's the more reason government should completely avoid the act of protecting the competition, an attitude that is common among corrupt governments, which through favoritism and interventionism create special platforms for some economic gangsters, giving space for corrupt officials and "crony capitalists" to control competition, and as a result, impede economic growth, for only a genuine competitive system tends to resonate with a high degree of economic opportunities.

THE NEED FOR EFFECTIVE INSTITUTIONS IN NIGERIA

Nigeria as a nation state has long made a transition from a largely controlled economic system to a market-oriented one, which is a result of the country's embrace of the capitalist system following the emergence of some effective and efficient institutional structures. More so, for human transactions to thrive, it's crucial to appreciate simple, stable, and universal ground rules for coordinating human conduct in the economy and establishing trust, creating institutions that can deploy appropriate effective sanctions. This is because the appropriate rules open life opportunities for all by creating predictability and security. Enterprising people can then concentrate on their own aspirations and capabilities without having to glance over their shoulders all the time to see whether their venture is imperiled by the next confiscation, the next arbitrary act by a corrupt official, the next prescriptive regulation, or the next lawless act by someone powerful.

Before now, Nigeria had been through decades of state management that produced nothing more than an inefficient economic system, which glaringly failed to deliver visible development in the country. It had almost completely destroyed the potentials for economic advancement and greatness of Nigeria. Nigeria experienced decades of military rule that had in no small measure hampered economic development, which evolves through market interaction.

This story is of three young men who went to the same higher institution in the northern part of Nigeria, grew to become successful in their chosen careers, and had at one time or another been in a position of high responsibility. One is a sitting governor in one of the northern states; the second is Nasir El-rufai; and the other Nuhu Ribadu. Their ability to exhibit uncommon courage, passion, and extraordinary commitment is legendary.

Assessed in reverse order, Ribadu seems to stand out as the strongest of the pack in terms of "guts." In a paper delivered on May 19, 2009, at St. Anthony's College, University of Oxford, Ribadu, as a visiting fellow at the Center for Global Development, the former executive chairman of the Economic and Financial Crimes Commission (EFCC) gave an in-depth analysis of capital loss and corruption in Nigeria. He made it clear to the panel that the effects and the disturbing implications of corruption in the global market is the same since the global economy is now highly integrated and interconnected and that the absence or lack of consistent, firm regulation and oversight in one place can undermine stability in another country far away. Without intending to malign his country, Nigeria, he claimed, "When you think of corruption, there will always be specific personalities and places that jump to mind, and inevitably Nigeria is near the top of that list." The question one asks, aside from the fact that corruption is not a native of any land, why it has taken an easier residence in Nigeria. The chaos is often permitted by systemic inefficient institutions and rules that carry sanctions.

I agree with Ribadu: societies that have been able to move ahead are those that put statutes in place to criminalize corruption and ensure that the enforcement mechanisms are proper and ready for action. He stated further that no attempt should be made to trivialize corruption, and as resources are stolen, confidence not just in democratic governance but in the idea of just leadership ebbs away. In this way, a culture of corruption is instituted, which destroys or undermines the capacity of the government, as an apparatus of the state to build credible, accountable institutions or put the right policies in place.

The African Union, according to Ribadu, reported that corruption drains the region of some $140 billion a year, which is about 25 percent of the continent's official GDP, and that, as a result of leadership chaos and frequent regime change, a general in one of the military regimes was believed to have taken for himself between $5 and $6 billion, investing most of it in the Western world. It was on this premise, coupled with the courage and passion to use the platform offered him by the government, that Ribadu developed his own project of positive change.

It was with this same background that EFCC, as the government's investigating apparatus in this regard, proceeded with the auditing of the serving state governors and public officials suspected of stealing public funds. Ribadu claims to have received great support from the London Metropolitan Police, in cases involving two former governors; one was found to have operated twenty-five bank accounts in London alone for the purpose of being able to juggle money and outsmart the law; while the other had four properties in London valued at about 10 million pounds, in addition to another property in Cape Town valued at $1.2 million. And according to Ribadu, "Two million pounds were restrained at the Royal Bank of Scotland in London and more than $240 million in Nigeria ... in addition to bank accounts traced to Cyprus, Denmark, the United States, and the Bahamas (Capital Loss and Corruption 2009, Paper presented at St Anthony's College, University of Oxford by Mallam Ribadu)."

Ribadu made a frightening revelation that between 1960 and 1999, Nigerian officials had stolen or wasted more than $440 billion.

That is six times the Marshal Plan, the total sum used to rebuild a devastated Europe in the aftermath of the Second World War. And he added, "When you look across a nation and a continent riddled with poverty and weak institutions, and you think of what this money could have done—only then can you truly understand the crime of corruption, and the almost inhuman indifference that is required by those who wield it for personal gain."

The summary of his discourse is to the effect that, when corruption is enthroned as king, it becomes impossible to demand accountability in leadership, and it diminishes our capacity to trust in authority. And when the situation of the society has become "everybody is on his own, while we all rely on the help of God," and when we lack the capacity and apparatus to require the government to address critical concerns that ail society, our ability to build stronger institutions becomes difficult if not impossible.

Ribadu posits that, "Corruption makes democracy impossible because it subverts the will of the people. A select few, with so much money and authority, continues to steal elections and make a mockery of the notion of government by the people or for the people (Ribadu 2009)."

Indeed, corruption, in Ribadu's view, is the greatest crime the world has ever known. And those who suffer the most of its gruesome implications are the least able to fight it, since their resources, health, well-being, and future have, through the same corruption, been stolen away.

While congratulating Ribadu for this effort, regardless of his obviously mixed optimism for Nigeria, and indeed Africa, it is important to submit here that the problem is being deepened by the fact that politicians and bureaucrats, though often more equipped with superior information regarding the task of national development driven by the establishment of effective institutions, do not put to use their superior knowledge. They exploit this privilege for their self-interest, as they often run government to suit their own purposes, often at the expense of its citizens. This problem becomes acute when ordinary citizens not only lack adequate education, they lack the material means to defend their rights and liberties to confront the officials. And since empathy and love as motivation that is obtained in small, intimate communities is not practicable in complex mass societies like ours, rules that ensure effective sanctioning are highly imperative.

The truth is, we need effective institutions in our socioeconomic life. For instance, in the global currency market, traders who transact billions of dollars do not write and sign formal contracts. They may live in different cultures and jurisdictions and cannot rely readily on the judiciary of one country to sort out conflicts over contract fulfillment. Yet they deliver on contract, even when this means a loss to them. This is because they would otherwise have a serious need to safeguard their reputation. And those who do not respect the rule of engagement in this regard lose their reputation in the global currency market and do not find contract partners, so often end up out of business in no time.

This is evidence that massive capital appreciation and prosperity could emerge through self-enforced rules, not to mention a judicious, consistent, and systemic application of a robust and effective institutions that effectively create order in human conduct, transaction, and enterprise, fostering confidence, justice, prosperity, and peace.

The benefits of effective institutions include

1. Expediting business and facilitating social interactions. They promote entrepreneurial behavior and drive a culture of creativity and innovative use of resources, and they advance the horizon of human knowledge through the development of new technology.
2. Creating a sense of security and facilitating a healthy platform for social contact.
3. Protecting individual spheres of freedom while constraining the use of power and undue coercion and demarcate the extent to which the autonomous pursuit of our own subjective purposes can go without infringing the freedom of others.

Without effective and appropriate institutional constraints, many would take liberty for granted, freedom would collapse, and man's inhumanity to his fellow man would increase, thereby causing life to return to the Hobbesian state of nature (Hobbes was an English philosopher and political theorist best known for his book *Leviathan* [1651], in which he argues that the only way to secure civil society is through universal submission to the absolute authority of a sovereign) where life is poor, nasty, brutish, and short.

4. Serving as a credible instrument for engendering peace within the society, and they help ward off conflicts. Where people with different backgrounds, exposures, experiences, and lifestyles pursue their different self-interests and purposes, it is inevitable that conflicts will occasionally arise; thus, effective institutions help us to deal with such conflicts and offer us the best way in practice to resolving them.

5. Serving to encourage people to conserve scarce resources, enabling them to effectively appropriate the limited resources to plan for their own future as well as those of their heirs and descendants.

Only when stable, predictable institutions provide long-term certainty will people accumulate human and physical capital and trust that they will in due course reap as returns. But even at that, it is important for us to lay bare the logic required for a sustainable economic development. To this end, let's turn our attention to the piece of work I did as my final year undergraduate long essay, focusing on its fifth chapter.

THE FIFTH CHAPTER OF MY UNDERGRADUATE THESIS

While not making attempt to digress from the critical discourse on the state of affairs in Nigeria, let's quickly dig into the meat of the last chapter of my undergraduate thesis. The thesis was titled "The Limits of the Logic of Pure Forms" and Chapter 5 was titled "Expanding the Frontiers of Logic for National Development." In this work, I made an attempt to take the enterprise of logic beyond academics into the national space in order to create platforms for the building of socioeconomic and political superstructure that will engender sustainable national development.

Indeed, logic in its entirety can be employed as a tool for national development. This stems from our earlier argument that over-concentrating logic on abstraction without engaging it to address quotidian human concerns will castrate logic and make it irrelevant. Over-abstraction renders thought irrelevant to human experience and indeed human society. What then is the use of any discourse that has no relation to ordinary human enterprise? We argue for an expansion of the frontiers of logic by not only giving a deeper consideration for the contexts of its propositions but making it intelligible to human thought for the purpose of national development. The question that quickly arises is, how then can logic be used for national development?

We have argued earlier that logic is both a science and an art, implying its applicability to science as well as to art. We live in a world where human freedom has been taken to the extreme. Man is traveling on the path back to the seemingly hypothetical Hobbesian state of nature. There are powerful countries in the world that have in their possession atomic bombs with the capacity to dissolve all humans to mere dust. Indeed, in Africa, there is a cold relationship between the leadership and its citizenry. While elected leaders are complaining that citizens are not showing an adequate sense of responsibility, the masses, on the other hand, are complaining of the leaders' looting and squandering of taxpayers' money and being nonchalant about their plight. This is a sorry state of affairs in our nation, which needs an urgent process of well-articulated programs for addressing the issues.

Suffice it to say there is a difference between development and progress: development does not always imply progress.

According to professor and author Ezekiel Ogundowole, development is multidimensional while progress is unidirectional. He posits thusly:

> When development lingers backward we speak of regress. When it is merely a rotatory, oscillating, and without any established trajectory we notice self-canceling motion, then we speak of development, movements without progress. In this sense, the development of a given object is said to be stagnant. It is when development represents a forward and upward-thrust movement that progress may be said to be taking place. Unlike development, it is a unidirectional process, not multidimensional. Progress represents in truth, a forward, an upward-thrust motion along an optimal trajectory. ("Science and Technology in Sustainable Development: an Ethical Paradigm" [PhD thesis])

He holds further, "Progress … is a realization in the field of economics, social life, politics and culture, a commendable general upliftment of the masses." In this connection, what we need as a nation is progress rather than a retrogressive self-canceling kind of motion or development, where a lot of activities take place but nothing really moves forward.

It is imperative that policymakers in Nigeria begin to use the instrumentality of logic to arrange priorities in such a way that there will be equipoise in our political and socioeconomic life. A coherent and consistent arrangement and rearrangement of policies, tailored toward progressive development of the citizens, is needed to enhance their psychological and intellectual capacity for national development. Hence, they would become enlightened people through tutelage in logic, which would make them assets to the country rather than a liability.

We conclude by saying that a tutelage in logic is needed, from the followers to the leaders, that will engender optimal progressive trajectory of development. Indeed, logicians must as a matter of responsibility bring logic to the understanding of the people. Every aspect of national affairs needs logic as a tool for enlightenment and progressive development. Therefore, logic as a discipline of depth and abstraction is much needed in this age.

Having said this, the purposes of progressive development as delineated by effective institutions must be considered on a regular basis in our national life. Without doubt, all odds seem to be against us, despite Nigeria's stupendous endowment in human and natural resources, indicating that national progress seems to be going south, especially given the massive increase in the army of unemployed youths in the country.

In 1963, Nigeria's population was about fifty-six million, a large percentage of which was employed until it began to decline in the early 1980s, despite the oil boom. The country appears to be moving forward, but her development is akin to an oscillating and a self canceling motion that ultimately tends backward while other countries are making progress. This shouldn't be, considering that unemployment truly costs the country a loss of about two trillion naira annually from the absence of commercial activities that should ordinarily have taken place. Thus if the government does not find a way to execute a careful "blue-ocean strategy," it will result in about sixty million Nigerians being gainfully employed, but it could take the nation two decades to bridge the existing job gap.

It seems much is being done, but little progress is being achieved to show for it. This is because of failure on the part of the leadership to position the nation in such a way that all government apparati are consistently deployed to create jobs and make available innovative platforms for creative endeavor. The country will continue to experience severe impediments in her journey toward economic development resulting from the wasting of human resources, leading to losses in terms of output, and, in turn, poorer income and increased poverty in the land. It require only a little imagination to understand this state of affairs would inhibit national cohesion and eventually result in national security challenges as currently being experienced in many parts of the country.

Indeed these critical socioeconomic concerns are already affecting Nigeria's global competitiveness. For instance, the country fell from 108th out of 175 countries in 2007 to 137 out of 183 countries in 2011 according to the IFC Ease of Doing Business Index. They ranked below Brazil, Morocco, Senegal, Egypt, Cameroon, and Gambia. What a self-canceling notion indeed! Nigeria's ranking in the World Economic Forum (WEF) Global Competitiveness Index has similarly dropped from 95 out of 131 countries in 2007 to the bottom 15 in the same year. The country is now ranked 127th out of 142 countries. Nigeria was ranked 128th out of 142 countries in terms of security, 135th in terms of infrastructure, and 140th in health and primary education quality. And Nigeria seems to be traveling further from the 2015 world's target for Millennium Development Goals for nations.

SOLUTION PROPOSED: A MARXIST TWIST TO GLOBAL CAPITALISM

The proposition here is predicated on what we've indicated earlier, where some corporate leaders have said their real assets are their people, the workers. Indeed, what Karl Marx had proposed concerning means of production and what should drive economic activity, namely the workers, has now come to reality, but in a dimension that even Karl Marx and most Marxists would find difficult to imagine.

The new source of wealth in the world today is intense intelligence and the ability to acquire and apply knowledge and know how, engaged for the purpose of creative entrepreneurship. Many organizations in the global arena as well as individuals are coming to the reality that their ultimate security lies more in their cognitive energy than in their real estate. We have transcended the age of agriculture, gone past the Industrial Age from which we proceeded to the Information Age.

Now we are in the age of Creation Intensification, and clever workers with clever machines are putting an end to mass organization.

Our problem, as a nation, is not in the denial that we face tremendous challenges but in the attitude toward commitment to bringing proactive, pragmatic, and sustainable solutions to these challenges. Without a doubt, Nigeria has all the potential for becoming a great nation, but it would require determination and great courage to unlock that greatness, as well as a passionate interest to depart from mere palliatives.

Inspired by this new thinking, Charles Handy, in his work *The Empty Raincoat* asserts categorically that, "If we are to cope with the turbulence of life today, we must start by finding a way to organize it in our minds ... until we do that we will feel impotent, victims of events beyond our control or even our capacity to understand." And if we manage properly the paradox we find ourselves in as a nation, we can't be held back from sustainable progress, not a self-canceling one.

The leadership and the managers of the state apparatus must become highly innovative by creating frameworks that will intelligently and clinically exploit our seeming contradictions as a people with diverse cultures, languages, experiences, and exposures to advantage and bring onboard stakeholders—that is, men and women who are creative thinkers, well-balanced in all ramifications of life, and have proven themselves credible in order to engage them in robust, productive dialectics, well-intended to create fundamental frameworks for aggregating in the most intelligent manner all the positive aspects of the African culture, and blend it with the emergent global culture of getting things done.

Even though the National Economic Empowerment and Development Strategy (NEEDS) document published in 2004 appears to be quite representative of our thrust of thinking, the leadership, however, seems to have lost the momentum. This is either from a result of political or personal exigencies being prioritized or from their lack of sincerity and commitment to hold a robust debate consistently with the citizens until the ideas contained in the document is appreciated, accepted, and established in the minds of the people, making them ready to cooperate with the government to execute its august propositions. But even at that, there is no guarantee of success as a result of years of lack of trust between the government and the people they govern. This is why we believe our proposition in this work is most pragmatic and results-oriented. And to this we now turn.

PANACEA FOR ECONOMIC RECOVERY: JOB CREATION, CREATIVE ENTREPRENEURSHIP

We hereby propose that policy documents or strategy that managers of state affairs have designed for economic recovery purpose must be focused on two things: one, massive creation of jobs; and two, creating a healthy environment and platforms for creative entrepreneurship to thrive, and indeed motivate the process to the point it becomes sustainable.

The worst affected in the problem of unemployment are adults between ages of twenty-one and forty who are the most energetic of the population, aside from the fact that they are the nation's future leaders. Government should tie all money spent on public expenditure to create sustainable employment by establishing formidable and consistent policies, and institutions that will regulate and close up all loopholes and corrupt practices that could frustrate this process.

Again, the government must pay genuine attention to sectors that have the potential to create the most jobs but have either been left untapped or redundant, such as tourism, commercialized agriculture, and education; and to engage a blue-ocean strategy that would make the informed sector more efficient, productive, profitable, and accountable. And should the government make definitive effort to create nothing less than three million jobs per annum, fifteen million jobs will be created for able-bodied men and women in five years; and if the government does this consistently for two decades, at least sixty million Nigerians will have been gainfully employed. This would trigger stupendous commercial activities and tremendous economic gain and development that comes as a result of effective and efficient engagement of the nation's human resources. As a result of this, the crime rate would nosedive since the higher number of the active population are profitably engaged, thereby reducing the national security problem; poverty will also be reduced beyond imagination, as the government uses the gains from increased tax revenue from the aggregation of the commercial activities to produce effective and efficient infrastructures that will improve the lifestyle of the citizens. Indeed, the government would increase her capacity to establish credible institutions of rules and effective sanctions.

The second proposition is to execute to the latter the mandate to create healthy platforms for creative entrepreneurship. It is the aggregation of the efforts of entrepreneurs who are actively engaged in small businesses and other innovative enterprises that can guarantee the production of 70 percent of new jobs, not the government or the large corporations. Besides, if the government would motivate this process genuinely, by removing obstacles to doing business and infrastructural constraints such as inadequate electric power supply and a dysfunctional and corrupt public services, while promoting small and medium enterprises, then more than a million new business with the capacity to employ at least two other people would emerge every year. The multiplier effect is that another three million people would actively and profitably be engaged, and nothing less than fifteen million people would have joined the workforce in five years. This would lead to massive economic growth.

Quo Vadis: Where Do We Go from Here?

CONGRATULATIONS. YOU'RE NEARLY finished reading this book. I trust it was laden with themes that engaged you with their pragmatism, practicality, emotionalism, and, at some points, comic relief. I trust we've also made an attempt to create a framework of action for you and/or your organization to operate in creative entrepreneurship. And in my candid view, this is the way to go, especially for citizens of emerging economies. Indeed, all African nations, especially those whose leaders have been unable to creatively turn the destiny of their human and social capital around for national gains, this book should be found useful. This book obviously doesn't offer you instant success but reveals that better things lie ahead. And so, this is the moment of truth, and it's absolutely instructive. I stumbled on this fundamental truth about life and human enterprise and made a promise to myself to use any platform available to me to communicate this truth.

MOMENT OF TRUTH: AVAILABILITY

This is your ability to be present when needed. Do not be fooled into thinking this is not imperative to your success in life or that it does not represent a veritable skill to be acquired. Indeed, of all the abilities one may develop, this might as well be the most important. How many great composers were there in the days of Mozart or after? How many do you know? You may know a dozen singers in your neighborhood with even better voices than some musicians who were making waves on the national scene just a few years back, yet not one of them is available to music-loving Nigerians. In other words, their music ability is no ability without presence. This is the same in every area of human enterprise.

After LeBron James led America's Dream Team to gold in the Beijing Olympics (2008), a common cart-pusher took him one-on-one in a basketball-skills contest and defeated him. He had more ability than LeBron, so to speak, but LeBron had availability. You need to develop your availability. You need to know how to show up at the right time. You need to learn how to volunteer for the dirty jobs, not because you are the dog but because you are developing your availability.

Ability has a way of magnifying when it is blended with availability.

David (in the Bible) would probably have remained just a shepherd boy with a great personal story of facing a lion one on one, but nobody would have celebrated him if he had not dared show up and confront Goliath. It is possible that among the armies of Israel camped that day for battle were men who had more exploits under their belts than David. They had more ability but failed to be available when it mattered most.

Not too long ago did the news of Dr. Louis Nelson's historic discovery of a cure for diabetes from herbs make the headlines. Do not be deceived by the name. Dr. Nelson is a full-blooded Nigerian who obtained his PhD from a Nigerian university (University of Ibadan). It can be said that his ability has met with availability as he has already registered his patent in the United States, and you can be sure with more than 123 million people suffering from the disease worldwide, he is made for life. Reason: He showed up; otherwise, that discovery could have graced his laboratory desk for the next hundred years without being celebrated. The cries that he just fed off years of research on traditional medicine only further highlight the point; ability is nothing without availability. Do you have a great idea resting majestically in your head, a great song yet to be sung, a great play or movie still unscripted, a great product that could redefine the banking industry, a great approach to Nigeria's power problems, a great solution to Africa's economic and conflict problems? These are great nothings and will remain so until they become available.

You must learn to show up. Develop the ability called *availability*. Be ready in season and out of season. Learn to be there when it matters most. Take a prominent role on your team. Dare to ask that question even if it may seem stupid; get the attention of the people who matter by bringing valuable solution to problems, tasks, concerns, or any challenge. Take the risk; the heavens will not fall. At worst, you will have to try again, but please be available. You can't win in a race where you are absent.

Indeed, your company's great customer service will remain a great nothing if you do not make it available to the customer when he needs it most. Your robust IT infrastructure will amount to nothing if it is not available to the customer who needs it. Your collective ability as a corporate entity will be nothing if it is not available to the customers. Remember the saying, "When the desirable is not available, the available becomes desirable."

It is for this reason that I made available to you this framework for success.

In the first chapter, it was made clear that new global platforms are now available for all those who care to exhibit discipline and the courage to take advantage of it and execute innovative ideas with robust energy in order to accomplish tremendous success, stupendous wealth, and massive global impact.

In chapter two we developed a new and innovative scientific approach to developing value-driven competence, called vacuum analysis technique. This technique was originally conceptualized by this author to increase your availability skill, either as a staff member or an associate in an organization or as owner or manager of an enterprise.

Chapters three and four were conceived to encourage the development of your faculty for entrepreneurship no matter how difficult, and to increase your capacity to grasp and utilize the platform of creative entrepreneurship, making available products that will solve some of the seemingly innumerable problems of human enterprise.

Chapter five was prompted by the need to explore the potentials in our social networks to advance our cause economically so we can fulfill our purposes in life without destroying or obstructing the fundament of nation building.

Then the sixth chapter was intended to advance the performance of our enterprise through modern digital devices as veritable tool that can help expand our capacity of developing sustainable availability skill in record time.

Lastly, not only because this author is an African and a concerned student of global affairs, or, above all, a citizen of the largest black nation in the world, Nigeria, it is imperative we consider the fundamental problems bedeviling the country, one of which is a phenomenon of inefficient institutions. This has led to deeply rooted corruption that has consistently weakened the nation's potential for greatness, and to devise an innovative and sustainable cure for this malady as she launch-pads herself for economic and social repositioning, and to be repositioned the country and Africa as a whole need vision, a lot of courage, objectivity in the midst of diversity, simplicity, a lot of sacrifice, purposeful patience, and a global outlook.

At this final curve, I am reminded of Charles Handy's story of his wife's ancestor, Sir Rowland Hill, famous for his invention of the penny post and the first postage stamps in the 1840s. He started out as a schoolteacher in his father's school. He was not rich, or famous, or influential, but he saw a problem that needed to be dissolved by his creative mind and decided he could not live with himself if he refused to do something about it. The problem was that prior to

Rowland Hill's campaign, it was only the rich who could afford to send real letters to each other. Letter writing was indeed an elite pastime. At this time, letters were priced according to their weight and the distance they had traveled and were paid for by the recipient.

And even though he was not in the postal service, nor had he any business with it, Rowland Hill proposed that cognitive thinking be directed toward this concern, that, "If every letter costs only one penny, no matter where it went to in Britain, and if it was prepaid by a 'stamp' which you could buy in advance and stick on," he argued that two things would happen: first, the volume of mail would expand hugely, more than compensating for any loss on the cost of the longer deliveries, but, more importantly, everyone would be able to send letters to each other. And according to him, this would encourage learning and national cohesion, as friends would be able to keep in touch with each other, mother with son, wife with her distant husband. And this for him would not just be a business enterprise but a vehicle for social transformation.

It took years of unrelenting campaigning and robust argument for the Parliament to believe and eventually execute Rowland Hill's proposition; and they experienced unprecedented results within a decade of operating on his proposal to the extent that fifty countries adopted the idea of pre-bought stamps, and the modern postal service was born. Rowland Hill died a rich and highly honored man, and he's remembered to this day as the father of the penny post. This is courage only common with authentic revolutionaries and creative entrepreneurs, who will consistently measure themselves scientifically with the vacuum analysis technique to ensure a value-driven competence in their affairs. They also benchmark the best in their industry and take further steps to launch into uncharted courses and undefined territories, creating new demand in the marketplace, inventing solutions to critical problems of humanity.

Inasmuch as we cannot all be social reformers, we also cannot wait for the mountains to move. We should approach the mountain with dignified courage and tenacity and climb it ourselves. We may not be able to proffer solutions to all human problems and predicaments within the limited time we have on this earth, but we must explore our full potentials, rise up to the legitimate task of an authentic revolutionary and creative entrepreneur, and continue to crack the code of possibilities in business and every other human enterprise.

GLOSSARY

Algorithm – is a process or set of rules to be followed in calculations or other problem-solving operations, especially by a computer.

Blue Ocean – is the creation of uncontested market space that makes the competition irrelevant. A Blue Ocean offers new opportunity for profitable and rapid growth to an entirely new market.

Brainpower – is the intelligence or Intellectual capacity of people with well-developed mental abilities.

Cash Cow – is a business jargon for a business venture that generates a steady return of profits that far exceed the outlay of cash required to acquire or start it, and can be used to boost a company's overall income and to support less profitable endeavors.

Cloud Computing – is the practice of using a network of remote servers hosted on the Internet to store, manage, and process data, rather than a local server.

Competitive Advantage – is the favorable position an organization seeks in order to be more profitable than its competitors: It involves communicating a greater perceived value to a target market than its competitors can provide, which can be achieved through avenues like offering a better quality product or service, lowering prices and increasing marketing efforts.

Complex Adaptive Systems – are special cases of complex systems, often defined as a complex macroscopic collection of relatively similar and partially connected micro-structures – formed in order to adapt to the changing environment, and increase its survivability as a macro-structure: It also refers to, any human social group-based endeavor in a particular ideology and social system such as political parties, communities, geopolitical organizations, war, and terrorist networks of both hierarchical and leaderless nature.

Corporate Management System (CMS) – is one of the most important parts of the infrastructure of any modern company, automating financial and logistics management functions: its implementation provides the full functionality necessary for analysis as well as management of financial, personnel, operational activities, and maintenance services of the enterprise, which forms a solid base for optimum solutions at all levels of management both at the present moment, and in the long-term.

Creative Entrepreneurship – is the practice of setting up a business – or setting yourself up as self-employed - in one of the creative industries. The focus of the creative entrepreneur differs from that of the typical business entrepreneur or, indeed, the social entrepreneur in that s/he is concerned first and foremost with the creation and exploitation of creative or intellectual capital. Essentially, creative entrepreneurs are investors in talent – their own or other people's.

Deregulation – is when economic "restrictions" (such as taxes, quotas, law to protect workers right, the environment, the welfare of the public) are repealed by the government, and a "free" market is advocated. Here, the government seeks to allow more competition in an industry that allows near-monopolies.

Emerging Economies – are nations with social and business activity in the process of rapid growth and industrialization, which is shown by some liquidity in local debt and equity markets and the existence of some form of market exchange and regulatory body.

Foreign Direct Investment (FDI) – is a direct investment into production or business in a country by an individual or company of another country, either by buying a company in the target country or by expanding operations of an existing business in that country.

Franchise – is an agreement between two legally independent parties which gives a person (the franchisee) the right to market a product/service using the trademark and trade name of another company (the franchisor). Through this agreement the franchisee has the right to market the product/service using the operating methods of the franchisor. The franchisee has the obligation to pay the franchisor fees for these rights and the franchisor the obligation to provide rights and support to the franchisee.

Ideation – is the creative process of generating, developing, and communicating new ideas, where an idea is understood as a basic element of thought that can be visual, concrete, or abstract. It comprises all stages of thought cycle, from innovation, to development, to actualization.

Industrial Revolution – is the transformation from an agricultural to an industrial nation.

Interventionism – is an economic position favoring interventions in the market in the public interest on behalf of government: Though a framework of market economy, it exist as a hampered market economy, informed by any act of government that both represents the initiation of physical force and, at the same time, stops short of imposing an all-round socialist economic system, in which production takes place entirely, or at least characteristically, at the initiative of the government.

Inventory Control – is the supervision of the supply and storage and accessibility of items in order to insure an adequate supply without excessive oversupply.

Joint Stock – is the stock or capital funds of a company held jointly or in common by its owners

Mass Market – is the market for goods that are produced in larger quantities, and also describe the largest group of consumers for a specified industry product.

Merger and Acquisition – is an aspect of corporate strategy, corporate finance and management dealing with the buying, selling, dividing and combining of different companies and similar entities that can help an enterprise grow rapidly in its sector or location of origin, or a new field or new location, without creating a subsidiary, other child entity or using a joint venture.

Millennium Development Goals – are eight international development goals that were established following the Millennium Summit of the United Nations in 2000, following the adoption of the United Nations Millennium Declaration. It's the result of a pledge made by 189 nations to free people from extreme poverty and multiple deprivations.

Outsource – is to obtain (goods or a service) by contract from an outside supplier; the contracting out of a business process to a third-party.

Prescriptive Regulation – is an approach to regulation that is based on adherence to explicitly prescribed action. This approach to regulation provides detailed specifications of rules and standard which must be followed and met.

Productive Capacity – is that portion of a work center's total capacity needed to process currently scheduled production, while **protective capacity** is additional capacity held in reserve to ensure that a sufficient quantity of parts can be manufactured to adequately feed the bottleneck operation. Protective capacity is, to some degree, a matter of opinion, for it can involve a substantial proportion of total capacity if a company intends to retain sufficient capacity to cover extremely large (and rare) production spikes. Conversely, if management is content to allow some occasional downtime at its bottleneck operation, then it may define protective capacity as a much smaller number.

Red Ocean Market – is where everyone is just talking a different version of the same thing to the same group of people versus a Blue Ocean where you guide new people over to your primary program. It is either when businesses enter an over-saturated marketplace, or they simply defend their current position.

Six Sigma – is a set of strategies, techniques, and tools for process improvement. It was developed by Motorola in 1981. It became famous when Jack Welch made it central to his successful business strategy at General Electric in 1995. Today, it is used in many industrial sectors.

Social Institution – is an organizational system which functions to satisfy basic social needs by providing an ordered framework linking the individual to the larger culture.

Sustainable Development – refers to a mode of human development in which resource use aims to meet human needs while ensuring the sustainability of natural systems and the environment, so that these needs can be met not only in the present, but also for generations to come.

TCP (Transmission Control Protocol) – is a set of rules (protocol) used along with the Internet Protocol (IP) to send data in the form of message units between computers over the Internet. While IP takes care of handling the actual delivery of the data, TCP takes care of keeping track of the individual units of data (called packets) that a message is divided into for efficient routing through the Internet.

Throughput – is the productivity of a machine, procedure, process, or system over a unit period, expressed in a figure of merit or a term meaningful in the given context, such as output per hour, cash turnover, numbers of orders shipped. In data communication – it is the measure of the efficiency of a network expressed as the data transfer rate of useful and non-redundant information, which depends on factors such as bandwidth, line congestion, error correction etc.

ACKNOWLEDGMENTS

I BINIKE IBIDOLAPO, MY wife, gave all, mentally, physically, financially, and psychologically to make the journey of this work from idea to reality possible, and I thank her for her honest feedback. I will eternally appreciate Mum for instilling in me the importance of integrity, humility, hard work, consistent lifestyle, and tenacity. I got tremendous support from Anthony Adejugbe, the Chairman/CEO of Tonique Oil Servicing, Andrew Akinola, a senior executive in Shell Petroleum Development Company Nigeria, my partners in Plectrum, Femi Akinlade and Patrick Durodola. My flair for creative entrepreneurship was inspired by my robust interactions with Damilola Ororo of PIT and Dayo Arowosaye of Cinch Strategies. Some fantastic men and woman of God have also inspired this work one way or another: Peter Abiola Adebisi, Myles Munroe, T.D. Jakes, Mike Murdock, Dele Adedeji, Poju Oyemade, Francina Norman, David Oyedepo, Chris Okotie, Femi Paul, and Dr. Daniel Olukoya, among others.

My exposure to global trends on developmental and political economy was greatly influenced by my interaction with Professor Pat Utomi through the platform of Centre for Value in Leadership, far before my training under the World Bank Group's sponsored Debate to Action on Sustainable Development. Professor Jide Oshuntokun, a former representative of Nigeria at the United Nation and the country's former ambassador to Germany, personally and specifically advised that I should always consider the implication of any work of mine as a tool for national development. Steve Ubimago, the copy editor at *Business World*, also gave superb guidance, making the book reader friendly and at the same time profound.

Finally, the following works of great repute have guided this book as a superior framework for creative entrepreneurship: *Corporate Canaries* (Gary Sutton); *Re-Imagine* (Tom Peters); *Blue Ocean Strategy* (W. Chan Kim); *The World Is Flat* (Thomas Friedman); *Execution* (Larry Bossidy); *Jack Welch on Leadership* (James W. Robinson); *Business at the Speed of Thought* (Bill Gates); *Good to Great* (Jim Collins); *The Empty Raincoat* (Charles Handy); and the seminar speech of Leke Alder, and Folusho Phillips among others.

BIBLIOGRAPHY

Appadorai, A. *The Substance of Politics*, Madras: Oxford University Press, 1975.

Bossidy, Larry and Ram Charan. *Execution*, London: Random House Business Books, 2002.

Collins, Jim. *Good to Great*, London: Random House Business Books, 2001.

_____. *How The Mighty Fall*, New York: HarperCollins Publishers Inc., 2009.

Fajolu, T. O. "Expanding the Frontiers of Logic for National Development," *The Limits of Logic of Pure Forms*, August 2005.

Foote, Nathaniel, Russell Eisenstat, and Tobias Fredberg. "How a New Breed of CEO Delivers Extraordinary Economic and Social Value," *Harvard Business Review*, September 2011.

Friedman, Thomas L. *The World is Flat*, London: Penguin Books, 2005.

Goleman, Daniel. *Social Intelligence*, New York: Bantam Dell, 2006.

Handy, Charles. *The Empty Raincoat*, London, Arrow Books, 2002.

Hartman, Jed. "Largest US Corporations," *Fortune 500*, May 2011.

Hill, Charles W. L. *Global Business Today*, New York: McGraw Hill, 2002.

Hill, Napoleon. *Think and Grow Rich*, New York: Penguin Group, 2007.

Kasper, Wolfgang. *Economic Freedom and Development*, Lagos, Dat & Partners Logistics Ltd, 2004.

Ijimakinwa, Feyi, "Availability," *Moment of Truth: Vol 2, 2009. Former weekly publication of the Corporate Communications Department of Wema Bank Plc.*

Kim, Chan W. *Blue Ocean Strategy*, Boston: Harvard Business School Publishing Corporation, 2005.

Maubossin, Michael J. "Embracing Complexity," *Harvard Business Review*, September 2011.

Ndubuisi, F. N. *Man and State*, Lagos: Foresight Press.

Peters, Tom. *Reimagine*, London: Dorling Kindersley Limited, 2003.

Ribadu, Nuhu. "Capital Loss and Corruption: The Example of Nigeria," testimony before the House Financial Services Committee, May 2009.

Robinson, James W. *Jack Welch and Leadership*, California: Prima Publishing, 2001.

Soubbotina, Tatyana P. *Beyond Economic Growth: An Introduction to Sustainable Development*, Washington: The International Bank for Reconstruction and Development/The World Bank, 2004.

Taiwo-Fajolu, Dolapo. "My Journey through Infertility to Motherhood." www.ibinike.blogspot.com, 2011.

Unah, Jim. *Fundamental Issues in Government and Philosophy of Law*, Lagos, Joja Educational Research and Publishers Limited, 1993.

Wattles, Wallace D. *The Science of Getting Rich*, New York: Penguin Group, 2007.

Wilson, Douglas. *5 Cities That Ruled the World*. Tennessee: Thomas Nelson, 2009.

ABOUT THE AUTHOR

AIWO FAJOLU IS a trained thinker, an author, a speaker, and a development consultant, tutored by the World Bank Group on sustainable development in developing countries. He has been involved in training for the federal government on its youth-empowerment campaign and family-life education. With keen interest in real estate, oil and gas, human resources training, and management consulting, Fajolu has created a concept of value-driven and execution-oriented competence development technique called vacuum analysis, which makes a lasting, positive, and progressive impact on staff and management. He also helps revitalize troubled local businesses by facilitating their partnership with global brands.

He was deeply involved in bringing a leader in Europe on UPS, Newave (a member of The ABB Group), into Nigeria, their largest and the only market in sub-Saharan Africa aside South Africa.

www.ingramcontent.com/pod-product-compliance
Lightning Source LLC
Chambersburg PA
CBHW030756180526
45163CB00003B/1044